ALSO BY ROHIT BHARGAVA

Personality Not Included

Likeonomics

Always Eat Left-Handed

Non-Obvious Megatrends

The Non-Obvious Guide to
Working Remotely

MARKETING & BRANDING

Without a Big Budget

IDEAPRESS
PUBLISHING

BY ROHIT BHARGAVA

IDEAPRESS
PUBLISHING

Cataloging-in-Publication Data is on file with the Library of Congress.

ISBN: 978-1-64687-045-5

Special Sales
Ideapress Books are available at a special discount for bulk
purchases for sales promotions and premiums, or for use
in corporate training programs. Special editions, including
personalized covers, a custom foreword, corporate imprints, and
bonus content are also available.

Non-Obvious® is a registered trademark of the Influential
Marketing Group.

2 3 4 5 6 7 8 9 10

Read this book to learn how persuasive marketing can tell your story in a way that breaks through the noise, helping you keep your current customers while attracting new ones. Marketing influences how people act and what they believe. This book will teach you how to shape both.

Is This Guide for You?

If you picked up this book, you are not a dummy.

Many business guides treat you like an idiot. Some even say so on the cover. This is not one of those books.

The **Non-Obvious Guides** all focus on sharing advice that you haven't heard before. This book is my contribution to the series, based on almost two decades of leading marketing strategy for some of the most recognizable brands in the world and then leaving to become an entrepreneur and start two businesses.

Like most of our authors, I would love to share these insights with you over coffee. Until I get that chance, this book aims to be the next best thing. I hope you find it entertaining and useful!

ROHIT BHARGAVA

Founder, Non-Obvious Guides

PART 2—EXECUTION

How to Read This Book

Throughout this book, you will find links to bonus worksheets, templates, and other resources designed to help you put the advice you'll read into action.

> **FOR ONLINE RESOURCES, VISIT:**
> **www.nonobviousguides.com/marketing**

Referenced in the book, you will also see these symbols which refer to content that will further your learning.

— FOLLOW THE ICONS: —

TEMPLATES
One-page templates to help you strategize.

DOWNLOADS
Useful further reading.

TUTORIALS
Detailed lessons on how to do a task.

VIDEOS
Videos to watch online.

CHAPTER SUMMARY
Key takeaways and important points

In this book, you will learn how to . . .

- ✓ Earn trust by being more believable in a skeptical world.

- ✓ Understand your customer's journey and how they think.

- ✓ Create a memorable logo and persuasive tagline to stand out.

- ✓ Use personality to engage your customers and build loyalty.

- ✓ Build a one-page marketing plan to promote your business.

- ✓ Strategically use social media, email, and the web without wasting your time.

- ✓ Stand out at a crowded trade show or industry event.

- ✓ Inspire your employees to promote your business.

- ✓ Adapt your strategy in a world fundamentally shifted by the global pandemic.

Introduction

A few years ago, Elon Musk launched a car into space.

The stunt was part of his SpaceX company's launch of the Falcon Heavy rocket, and it grabbed worldwide attention. After all, who could ignore a photo of a mannequin sitting in a Tesla Roadster orbiting high above the earth?

One media property even described it as "the greatest ever car commercial without a dime spent on advertising." The stunt was perfectly in character for Musk, too.

He once bragged to a reporter about doing more than $1 billion in sales with no marketing, no advertising, and no sales force. This is the dream. If you can create a great product or a stellar experience, then all your marketing should happen effortlessly and without a budget, right?

The truth is marketing rarely works out like that.

In fact, it didn't work out like that for Musk, either. While he might not have spent anything on traditional advertising, launching the car into space was a highly calculated and costly marketing stunt designed to inspire the same awe and curiosity that he aims to awaken with his products.

> Marketing is how you share the story of your business with the world to inspire belief and encourage action.

For Musk, making you believe that his company can accomplish the impossible is part of the brand. It helps him sell more cars because many Tesla buyers feel as if they are doing their part to change the world and save the environment.

Although he probably would never describe himself this way, Elon Musk is a master marketer. I should know. I'm obsessed with marketing.

WHY NO ONE WATCHES TV WITH ME

I see marketing everywhere, and I can't help paying attention to it.

I watch the promotional messages before a YouTube video even after the "Skip Ad" button appears. I take photos of the interesting disclaimers on restaurant menus. Most members of my family refuse to watch TV with me because I rarely fast-forward through the commercials. I once nearly missed a flight because I started talking with an airport store owner about her marketing and lost track of time.

While I consume all this marketing, I build campaigns and strategies in my head. I imagine new ways for a business to tell its story every time I walk by. And I feel bad when I see great opportunities wasted.

For me, this fascination with marketing has been years in the making.

HOW I BECAME AN ENTREPRENEUR

After leaving my agency job more than five years ago, I started my first business with my wife, and a year later we started a second one. For each business, we had to build a brand, develop a marketing strategy, devise ways to attract and retain customers, and sell a service for one and a physical product for the other.

Along the way, I discovered that many things I thought I knew about marketing were wrong.

Instead of working with million-dollar advertising budgets, I was now an entrepreneur with a non-existent marketing budget.

So my thinking changed. I started working faster and avoiding waste. I focused on what succeeded and ignored everything else.

Within a few years, my first business surpassed $1 million in revenue. A year later, the second did the same. Then when the pandemic hit, we quickly pivoted both businesses to not only survive but continue to grow despite the global business downturn. More importantly, we shifted our marketing strategy to prepare for a time when the pandemic would end and we would get back to a "future normal."

What was our secret? How did a traditional marketer like me reinvent the "big company" approach to prosper without relying on big spending?

I wrote this book (and updated this Second Edition!) to answer those questions.

PART ONE

Strategy

CHAPTER 1

The Modern Crisis of Believability

Twenty years ago—just as the Internet started to gain popularity—a team of researchers from Rice University decided to study how people consumed websites. While watching their subjects, they were surprised to see that nearly everyone avoided looking at the website areas reserved for banner ads.

The effect was so severe that researchers coined a term to describe it: **banner blindness.**[1] It should have been a warning for anyone doing marketing as well because it illustrated a scary fact:

> People hate marketing so much they often create an intentional "blindness" to avoid it.

Today you can create temporary email addresses to avoid spam, block ads, and mask your identity and location online. Social media automatically filters out messages that don't align with your interests, political beliefs, and worldview.

The more people learn to ignore what they don't find relevant, entertaining, or helpful, the harder you have to work to earn their attention. How can you navigate this skepticism and promote your business? The first step to rising above it is to understand why people have become so skeptical in the first place.

To do that, let's take a quick jump back in time.

1.1 Cowboys, Ad Men, and Evil Marketing

In the 1950s, Darrell Winfield was about to become famous. While you might not know his name, you probably recognize the character he portrayed: the Marlboro Man.

The advertising campaign featuring Winfield as an iconic cowboy who loved Marlboro cigarettes ran for more than 20 years. It continued despite mounting evidence that the product he promoted was killing its customers.

The campaign led people into the '60s and '70s—a golden age of marketing and manipulation by advertising executives who shaped public perceptions on everything from Kodak film to German cars.

As *Mad Men* inspiration Jerry Della Femina famously joked, "Advertising is the most fun you can have with your clothes on." If you spent the right amount and had the right message, you could influence public opinion on a mass scale.

During the 80s and 90s, advertising started to dominate television and expanded to digital media in the form of banner ads and emails. Many consumers started to see marketing as the enemy—a force whose goal was to use interruptions to sell something, even if it meant playing on their fears and insecurities.

Over the past 20 years, in many ways marketing has gotten worse. Whether it's blatantly exaggerated "natural" food packaging claims or fashion and beauty advertising designed to make you feel inadequate, the flood of unbelievable marketing we all face makes it harder for any brand or message to stand out.

This history of increasingly manipulative marketing played a big part in creating a culture where people are wary of trusting anything they see, hear, touch, taste, or smell. Yet this is not the fault of marketing alone.

| **1.2** | **How Fake News Makes** |
| | **Our Lives Harder** |

People now get their news from angry commentators or snarky comedians who offer an angle to every story. These days all news seems biased by politics or tainted by personal opinions.

The truth has a media problem.

The Internet lets anyone share an uncensored message, and has created an ocean where polluted information rises to the top and lies get presented as truth. Social media and every new cycle of political elections continually make it worse.

You can't take something bad off the Internet. That's like trying to take pee out of a swimming pool.

—Grant Robinson, *Blogger*

Consider these recent story headlines:

→ "Chocolate Milk May Be Better Than Sports Drinks for Exercise Recovery"

→ "Why Hollywood Doesn't Cast [insert any actor's name] Anymore"

→ "Chemical in McDonald's Fries Could Cure Baldness, Study Says"

→ "Bargain Teddy Bear Offer Sparks Violent Scenes Across Britain"

→ "87-Year-Old Trainer Shares Secret to Losing Weight"

→ "Sassy Seal Accidentally Slaps Man Across Face with an Octopus"

Even though headlines like these are misleading, they are also hard to resist because they engage our curiosity.

Click-bait headlines are changing our media consumption habits because we constantly must determine what is worth paying attention to. This combination of manipulative media and marketing has created what I call our *modern believability crisis*. Building trust or being believed is harder than ever before.

1.3   Three Reasons Consumers Distrust Everyone (Including You)

The media and marketing worlds share much of the blame for the believability crisis. But how did it happen? Here are three contributing factors that have shaped our disbelieving world today:

The inflated claims on this box led to a false advertising lawsuit.

1. **Real spin and actual lies:** Every time we see a breakfast cereal that supposedly boosts our immunity or vitamins that are "scientifically proven" to increase our lifespan, our skepticism of all marketing grows. Claims that seem too good to be true often are.

2. **Facelessness and corporate speak:** Many organizations use language that is regulated by lawyers and hence sounds robotic and distant. People only trust what they can understand.

3. **Media bias and fragmentation:** With much of our news coming from biased sources, the sad reality is that people are choosing media that reinforces their own beliefs and ignoring the rest.

Believability is a hard standard to meet today. After all, an individual business can't reinvent people's attitudes toward all marketing or media. The challenge reminds me of this joke I once heard:

> *Two boys are camping when they see a large,*
> *angry bear ready to attack. One boy calmly bends*
> *down to tie his shoes while the other looks at him.*
> *"What are you doing? You can't outrun a bear!"*
> *he says. The first boy replies, "I don't have to*
> *outrun the bear. I just have to outrun you."*

Clearly this isn't a story of loyal friendship, but it is a lesson for your business. In a skeptical world, the key to winning is being more trustworthy than the competition.

1.4   How to Be More Believable

When I wrote my first book, *Personality Not Included*, I explored the idea that consumers trust companies that are able to act more authentically. I interviewed nearly a hundred business owners and professionals. Together they demonstrated that the more a brand of any size promoted its personality and generated a human connection, the more trustworthy the brand was perceived to be. The brands that earned this trust sold more, had more loyal customers, and stayed in business longer.

How can you do the same thing? Here are a few tips:

TIP 1 TALK LIKE A REAL PERSON

I once read an interview in which the CEO of a large company defended himself by saying, "There was no nefarious activity. There wasn't any desire to obfuscate or hide information." Does this sound like someone you would trust? If you want to be believable, talk like a human—not a contract lawyer.

TIP 2 SHARE YOUR STORY

When fast-growing online T-shirt retailer Custom Ink talks about their brand, the story starts with one of their founders spending "long hours on his green couch," a hand-me-down from his big brother. Such personal details bring the struggles of starting the company and overcoming its growing pains to life. People trust stories they can relate to.

TIP 3 BE UPFRONT AND HONEST

If someone didn't ask, would you share the one thing you don't do so well? Being candid about your weaknesses is hard, and most of us are reluctant to do so. When we started our publishing company, one of our founding principles was to be upfront and honest.

Sometimes I would start conversations with authors by sharing what we are not so good at. Very quickly, our authors realized that we would never exaggerate our abilities. Now when we say we can do something, our authors always believe us.

**CHAPTER SUMMARY
KEY TAKEAWAYS:**

- Biased media and manipulative marketing have led us into the midst of a *modern believability crisis*.

- Most consumers today will be skeptical of your brand on their first encounter, so you must earn their trust.

- Focusing on authenticity and sharing the truth proactively are the keys to building trust.

CHAPTER 2

How to Create a Marketing Strategy

Next to an abandoned basketball court on Chicago's South Side, an unremarkable door looks as if it might lead to a tiny apartment building. Inside is one of the most unusual and extravagant dining experiences in the entire city.

EL Ideas, named for Chicago's elevated public transit system, challenges nearly every convention of a typical high-end restaurant.[2]

Renowned chef Phillip Foss, who boasts an impressive resume having worked at some of the most famous restaurants in the world, delights in doing things a bit differently. With an open kitchen and only 20 or so diners per seating, he serves the first dish of his $155 tasting menu without any utensils.

The cutlery-free course is caviar served on a glass plate—and as diners look around in confusion, Foss reveals that the way to eat it is to lick it off the plate. The plate licking is a bonding experience meant to loosen up the entire room. Who can take themselves too seriously after doing that in public?

VISIT ONLINE RESOURCES FOR:
A slightly embarrassing video of me doing some plate licking at EL Ideas.

This is the entrance lobby for EL Ideas restaurant.
→

The rest of the evening continues to challenge culinary traditions. Foss wears a blue button-down apron that makes him look more like an auto mechanic than a Michelin award-winning chef. Patrons are invited into the kitchen to watch his team in action at any time during the meal.

The experience at EL Ideas is about much more than that caviar dish. From the entrance to the kitchen staff, the food presentation, and even the unusual invitation for diners to bring their own wine instead of having a house wine list with a hefty markup—every choice is intentional.

The one thing that Foss and his team don't do is create a strategy around a single menu item.

2.1	## Why You Don't Need a Chicken Strategy

While each dish is important, a restaurant focusing on how to serve chicken would be like a coach focusing on how to tie players' laces to win a football match. This is what I call a chicken strategy: the error of focusing on a small and relatively insignificant detail instead of the bigger picture.

No great restaurant builds an experience on a single dish.

If you ever sat down and thought, "We need a Facebook strategy," that's an example of similarly small thinking. Focusing on just one platform or element of your business is like EL Ideas concentrating on a chicken (or caviar) strategy.

The restaurant meal is a theatrical production, and everything from how the food is prepared to how your senses are engaged is something that you can't help raving about, as countless people do online and in real life after the experience. Great marketing strategy always focuses on an experience, not a menu item.

2.2 The World's Most Common Marketing Mistake

When it comes to creating a marketing strategy, the worst way to start is by setting a budget.

Budgets can work a lot like deadlines. If you set a deadline for next Friday, you are virtually guaranteeing that your task will not be done until then. Most of us struggle to get a head start or spread a task out over time. Despite our best intentions, we almost never finish early.

Tasks will expand into the time you give them. Marketing budgets will do the same thing.

When you set a budget, you unintentionally create pressure to spend that money, whether it is smart and effective or not. This is one of the most common marketing mistakes by companies of all sizes.

Large companies waste millions of dollars on marketing and advertising because they spend money on the same things as in previous years. Their marketing is a habit instead of a strategy. And they know that they need to spend their designated budget, or the next year's budget will shrink.

When you have a marketing budget of $10 million, spending any less seems like a failure. The same thing can happen with $1,000.

A better way to calculate your marketing budget is to consider what you want to do with it and *what you want it to do for you.* And if it is working, your marketing budget could be unlimited. Here's how:

CASE STUDY: $1 MILLION MARKETING BUDGET

What if you could predictably generate $300 in profit for every $100 you spent on marketing? Here's how the math could work:

Cost of advertising = $100
Products sold from advertising = 50 units

Cost of goods = $2 per product ($100 cost of product)
Sales price for product = $10 per product ($500 total revenue)

Profit = $300 (total revenue minus cost of product and minus cost of advertising)

In this scenario, when you spent $100, you generated $300 in profit after accounting for all your costs. If you could keep this performance ratio constant, spending $1 million in advertising would generate $3 million in profit. Now you have a million-dollar marketing budget.

Note to the reader: This scenario makes the optimistic assumption that your sales stay constant as you increase your spending on marketing, which is not always the case.

2.3   The Value of Being Different

If you don't start your marketing plan by setting a budget, what should you do instead?

The best way to start a marketing plan is to understand how your business stands out from the competition. In Chapter 4, we will focus on the art of positioning, which involves finding the things that help you stand out from your competitors and be memorable to your customers.

Understanding what makes you different is always the ideal place to start your marketing plan. How can you decide where or even how much money to spend if you don't know what you're going to say?

> *Being the best isn't enough if nobody cares.* 🙶
> *Different is better than better.*
>
> —*Sally Hogshead*

We often think about being different in terms of better or cheaper. The problem is that such differences can fade. You might have a better location, selection, or price today, but that can change quickly.

The smarter way to stand out is by being unique. To see how this works, let's look at the story of a small dry-cleaning company.

STORY: HANGERS DRY CLEANERS

Some dry cleaners try to promote themselves as being better—your clothes done the same day by 5 p.m.! Others focus on being cheaper—your shirts done for $1.99 each!

Hangers, a small chain of dry cleaners based in Kansas City, Missouri, focuses on being different. Its key differentiator is using vans to pick up and drop off customers' dry cleaning. Unlike most competitors, Hangers also uses colorless and odorless liquid carbon dioxide to clean clothes, instead of toxic chemicals.

These choices are supported by quirky marketing such as returning clothing on hangers with funny taglines such as "In the closet and proud" or "You're the 23rd person I've seen naked." Such genuine personality, along with the convenience of home pickup and delivery, has helped Hangers operate profitably in a highly competitive and often commoditized industry for more than a decade.

2.4 How to Craft Your Non-Obvious Marketing Strategy

Hangers knows that being better or cheaper at cleaning clothes is not enough. What sets the chain apart is legendary convenience delivered through the radical idea of picking up and delivering dry cleaning to a customer's home or office. No one else does that, and even if competitors tried, it would take them a lot of resources to replicate the fleet of vans and the brand that Hangers has built.

This is what a real competitive advantage looks like: something that not only helps you stand out as different, but it's also done in a way that would be difficult for someone else to duplicate.

What the Hangers example also teaches is that the best marketing strategy must start with a distinctive answer to this question:

> What is the one thing you offer that is different *and* that your audience cares about?

The key here is that you need to be different *and* desired. Being different in a way no one cares about just makes you weird, and that's not ideal.

Here's a chart to illustrate this principle:

ORDINARY *Highly desired but not different*	**NON-OBVIOUS** *Different AND Desired!*
STUPID *Not desired or different*	**WEIRD** *Different but not desired*

DESIRED

DIFFERENT

As you think through the right way to differentiate your business, be careful that you don't lean too heavily on outside perspectives. There will be lots of people who have an opinion to share. Just remember you need to remain laser focused on what your customer actually cares about - not what your stakeholders or team members think.

© marketoonist.com

In the next few chapters, we will explore how you can craft your best answer to this question and build it into an effective marketing strategy.

To start, you will first need to build a better understanding of your customers, so we will focus there next.

**CHAPTER SUMMARY
KEY TAKEAWAYS:**

- The most common marketing mistake is setting a marketing budget before determining what you are going to say.

- A great marketing strategy always aligns with business strategy. Everything else follows from that.

- The best way to set your business apart is to focus on being different in a way that matters to your customers.

CHAPTER 3

How to Understand Your Customer

When Maura McCarthy first thought about her target audience, she pictured hip 30-somethings looking to settle down in their first home. As the co-founder of a modern homebuilder called Blu Homes, it seemed like a logical audience.

Instead, the company's first customer turned out to be a 60-something woman from Rhode Island. As McCarthy shared in an article for *Inc.*, it turned out these older consumers were a much better homebuyer for Blu Homes. They knew what they wanted, were affluent, and decisive.[3]

She described them as "green grandmas." The entire experience, McCarthy concluded, was a reminder that sometimes you must accept that your assumptions about your audience are wrong—and adapt.

3.1 How to Think Beyond Demographics

Do you know who *your* audience really is?

The most common way to describe them is by their age and gender, but this is hardly ever enough.

How much do you think a married, 30-year-old graphic designer and father of 2 young children has in common with a single, gay 19-year-old male studying engineering in college? Probably not a lot, yet they fall into the same 18-35 age demographic.

> Demographics are an outdated way to describe an audience.

The idea of a "green grandma" as a customer is a better example. While the term *grandma* does indicate that the buyer is female and older, the *green* adds an important descriptor. It tells you that customers care about the environment, are future oriented, and have a modern mindset.

Using only demographics to decide how to reach your customers is like buying a car based only on the color. To get the full picture, you need to look deeper.

3.2 The Benefits of Stereotyping Your Customers

Stereotypes can be a bad thing. The worst are racial stereotypes that reinforce biases and encourage discrimination. The definition of a stereotype is "a widely held but fixed and oversimplified image or idea of a particular type of person."

In marketing, sometimes an "oversimplified" image of an audience is exactly what you need—as long as you are using it to better understand an audience instead of excluding or judging people. For example, I recently read an article about traveling to Athens. It was offering suggestions for experiences tailored to five types of travelers: the First Timer, the History Buff, the Night Owl, the Island Hopper, and the Design Aficionado.

The lists of activities in the article were interesting because they catered to the passions and interests of each type of traveler. More importantly, the article recognized that one traveler might fit several of these stereotypes in different moments.

The bottom line is that demographics are not enough. To better understand your customers, you need to describe their common behaviors and beliefs.

CASE STUDY: UNDERCOVER PRINTER

Amy Zydel, the founder of Undercover Printer, describes her customers with a single word: procrastinators. Most of her orders come with rush deadlines from people who wait until the last moment. Rather than complain about the unrealistic demands, she built her business by embracing this behavior and becoming the "procrastinator's choice." The message in her marketing is the same: Even if you wait until the last minute, Undercover Printer can help get the job done.

3.3   How to Create a Customer Persona

The most comprehensive way to describe your audience is through writing a *customer persona*—a narrative description of a segment of your audience, written in a way that appears to describe a single individual. It is not a list of bullets or data points.

The hard part of writing good personas is to avoid using meaningless generalizations or resorting to stereotypes. This cartoon illustrates just a few of the most common missteps.

© marketoonist.com

So how can you write actually meaningful personas? Make sure they answer these questions:

1. What values do these people have, and how do they describe themselves?

2. What are their hobbies or favorite activities?

3. Where do they get their information, and how do they consume media?

4. What are their pain points, and how urgent is it for them to find a solution?

5. What would make them happy and meet their needs?

To bring this concept to life, let's review the customer persona for a reader of the *Non-Obvious Guide* series (like you!) that my team and I developed. See if this person sounds familiar.

EXAMPLE:
ARYA: THE "TIME-STARVED DOER"

Arya is about to start something new. She is curious, ambitious, and willing to learn—but doesn't have a lot of time for it. Her title doesn't define her—nor does her age. If there is anything that defines her, it's the belief that she's smart enough to learn just about anything quickly. She is no dummy. Yet she doesn't describe herself as an expert at everything and knows sometimes she needs help.

As a constant consumer of media, gaining her trust is hard. Skepticism is second nature to her, and anyone who promises miracles or offers a solution that is too good to be true is usually dismissed as untrustworthy. She has seen more than her fair share of bullshit, and she has a deep faith in her ability to detect and avoid it.

The one thing she does trust is a credible expert who doesn't try to flaunt their accomplishments. When confronted with the need to get advice, she will seek out people who are knowledgeable enough to have a point of view and humble enough to share it freely. Given a choice, she will always choose to have a coffee meeting to pick the brain of a mentor above any other form of learning.

If a book could come close to offering that type of experience, she would be the first to read it.

As you can see from this persona, we describe how our reader "Arya" sees herself (smart enough to understand any topic quickly), her worldview (skeptical and able to spot bullshit), how she gets information (consumes media constantly), and what would meet her needs (learning directly from a generous mentor).

All these details help our authors (including me) remember who we are writing for and to match our tone in these books to this persona. Creating your own customer persona description can help you do the same thing.

3.4	**How to Empathize with Your Customer**

The best customer persona comes from having a deep empathy for the people you want to reach. To help build your understanding of your customers, here are a few tips.

TIP 1 LEARN THE UNDERLYING NEED

Pregnancy tests typically are sold in two formats. The first helps track ovulation and fertile times. It contains 20 tests and includes a picture of a cute baby on the box. It is for the person who is trying to become pregnant.

The second "detects" pregnancy, offers fast results, and includes just two tests. The package looks more clinical and doesn't have a baby on the box. It is for the person who may or may not be trying to get pregnant and just wants a quick, accurate test result. Because the underlying needs are so different, the products are marketed and packaged differently.

Two examples of very different packaging.

TIP 2   ENGAGE IN "HATE-SURFING"

The Internet is the world's most irresistible complaint box—filled with negative comments. "Hate-surfing" describes the act of reading these negative comments to better understand what *not* to do—and how to perhaps solve some of those issues.

Southwest Airlines recently built its entire marketing strategy around the tagline "Bags Fly Free" after reading online complaints reinforcing the truth that every traveler hates paying additional bag fees. The transformed marketing campaign aligned with Southwest's business strategy of being the most traveler-friendly airline in the business.

TIP 3   OBSESS OVER YOUR EXPERIENCE

Sam Walton, the founder of Walmart, was famously arrested in Brazil inside a competitor's superstore because police found him on his hands and knees measuring the distance between the aisles. It was part of his obsession with optimizing every aspect of the retail experience. When was the last time you tried to buy your own product or consult your own customer service? Or measure your competitor's aisles (literally or figuratively)? Empathy comes from a true understanding of how you are serving your customer and a dedication to improving it—even if it lands you in a Brazilian jail.

3.5   The Five Phases of a Customer Journey

Your customers will take a journey to purchase your product. Along the way, they will figure out they have a need, discover your solution, evaluate it, compare it with others, decide to buy, and finally experience your product.

One tool to better understand this path is a *customer journey map*. It's a visual depiction of the process most customers go through when choosing to work with you or to buy your product.

If you want to understand how animals live, you don't go to the zoo; you go to the jungle.

—Martin Lindstrom, Author and
Consumer Researcher

 VISIT ONLINE RESOURCES FOR:
Watch my video interview with Martin Lindstrom about his insights and research.

When large brands do this, they often engage an expert to get permission to go and observe customers in their homes. Living in your customers' homes to observe them probably doesn't sound appealing to you (or your customers)! The good news is, most customer journey maps include a similar list of five phases:

1. **Discovery:** How do customers find out about you or discover they have a need?

2. **Evaluation:** How will customers make comparisons and review their options before buying?

3. **Purchase:** What is the process of making the purchase and receiving the product or service?

4. **Experience:** How and with whom is the product or service used, and how do they benefit?

5. **Advocacy:** How likely are those customers to talk about their experience?

Here is a template for mapping your own customer journey:

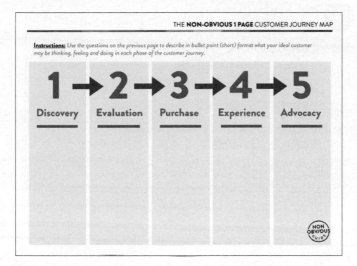

If you use this customer journey map alongside a good written customer persona, you can form a complete picture of your audience.

VISIT ONLINE RESOURCES FOR:
A downloadable template to help you map out your customer's journey and how to reach them.

**CHAPTER SUMMARY
KEY TAKEAWAYS:**

- Demographics are mostly meaningless. Age and gender only begin to describe your customers.

- A customer persona helps detail your audience's beliefs, interests, passions, and needs.

- The five phases of the customer journey are discovery, evaluation, purchase, experience, and advocacy.

CHAPTER 4

How to Position Your Business

One summer, I spent a forgettable four hours in Key West, Florida.

It was a short stopover from a cruise, and the bus ride into town took us past the main street, where shop owners lined up and yelled to attract us to their souvenir shops. Nearly everyone held a handwritten cardboard sign that promised the same deal: $5 T-shirts. Not surprisingly, no one on our bus seemed interested in a great discount on poorly designed, cheaply printed T-shirts.

At the opposite end of the main street was a store called the Key West Toy Factory. Inside they offered an open play area, unique toys, and a live magician. They sold $20 T-shirts, but the store's experience made up for the steeper price. And the people in our group ended up spending money there because it offered a unique experience worth remembering.

Would you rather be yelling at your customers from across the street or selling the same product at four times the price? This is why differentiation and positioning matters, and in this chapter, you'll learn how to do both for your business.

4.1   Why Positioning Matters

It is not enough to do something different or even to *be* different. None of that matters if your customers don't *realize* how you are different. Positioning is about differentiating yourself in the consumer's mind.

> Marketing without positioning is like winking at someone in the dark. You know what you're doing, but no one else does.

So how can you do this? Positioning starts with focusing on a few questions:

→ What is the one thing you offer that is different and that your audience cares about?

➔ When your best customers buy from you, what do they like most that keeps them coming back?

➔ Why do new customers decide to purchase from you or work with you?

As you go through answering these questions, you might face a moment of panic. *What if you're not actually that different from your competitors?*

You are not alone. Most every business owner has had that thought at some point. Worrying you are not unique is usually a crisis of confidence, not positioning.

Positioning requires belief in your business and the uniqueness of what you sell.

> If you don't think you're different, then no one else will either.

If, however, you are still trying to find what that real difference is and how to describe it, then this chapter will help.

4.2 The Five Elements of an Effective Marketing Message

The way to bring your positioning to life is through a marketing message. Sometimes called a *tagline*, good marketing messages share five core elements. A good marketing message should be:

1. **Tangible:** Is the actual benefit for customers understandable and real?

2. **Clear:** Does the message make sense, and is it in a language that customers understand?

3. **Relevant:** Will the target audience care about the message, and does it address their needs?

4. **Original:** Is the message unique and something that people haven't heard before?

5. **Elegant:** Are you sharing the message with well-chosen and meaningful words?

To see how each of these points can be applied, let's look at a few good examples of marketing messages that you might recognize.

ELEMENT	EXAMPLE	WHY IT WORKS
Tangible	"When It Absolutely, Positively Has to Get There Overnight" (FedEx)	Focuses perfectly on FedEx's capability to deliver overnight and their reputation for reliability.
Clear	"Compare Hundreds of Travel Sites at Once" (Kayak)	Straightforward message that relays exactly what the site does for you and the benefit you will get.
Relevant	"When You Care Enough to Send the Very Best" (Hallmark)	Positions Hallmark cards as the ultimate symbol of caring and rationalizes why their cards are more expensive.
Original	"Shave Money. Shave Time." (Dollar Shave Club)	Uses a creative play on words to clearly communicate the customer benefits they offer.
Elegant	"Open Happiness" (Coca-Cola)	Perfectly relays a double meaning—the emotion you feel when you open a Coke and the idea that happiness is available for anyone.

4.3 How to Write Your Tagline

A tagline is a short phrase that communicates the most important element or essence of your brand. We encounter them all the time—and they are easy to remember. *Just Do It. A Diamond Is Forever. Don't Leave Home Without It. Open Happiness.*

You probably know which brand is behind each of those taglines.

But what if you don't have a small army of branding consultants ready to spend months working on this for you? Can you really create an effective tagline like those for your business or message without a big budget?

The answer is yes, and here's a step-by-step process you can follow to do it.

STEP 1 CREATE A LIST OF WORDS

Make an audio recording of yourself describing your business to a friend or family member, and then listen back in order to write down the words and phrases you commonly use. Start with your sales pitch and focus on how you would persuade a prospective customer to work with you.

STEP 2 USE BORING DESCRIPTIVE PHRASES

Take your list of words and start to put them together into short phrases that could inspire a tagline. It could range from two words to a short sentence. The point here is to keep it boring and literal. The phrases you create at this stage should feel descriptive and true to your business. You can always focus on making it more original and creative later.

STEP 3 EVOLVE PHRASES INTO TAGLINES

Pick a few of your tagline ideas and start refining them. Now is when you can focus on the words you use and the ways you use them. One of my favorite resources to find better words and phrases for taglines at this stage is a book called *Words That Sell* by Richard Bayan. In it he offers more than 6,000 words or phrases to help you craft better marketing messages.

EXAMPLE: HOW TO CREATE A TAGLINE

Here is the step-by-step model for creating a tagline applied to this book series you are reading now. We used the same process described in this chapter to develop our branding and messaging for the *Non-Obvious Guides* series.

Step 1—Create a List of Words

Real, authentic, conversational, easy to read, short, useful, genuine experts, no fluff, not formulaic, down-to-earth, compilation, simple guide

Step 2—Use Boring Descriptive Phrases

Real experts giving real advice; Easy to read; Advice that works; Just like talking to an expert in person; Advice you have tried to find on Google; For smart people, not idiots

Step 3—Evolve Phrases into Taglines

A Guide You've Been Googling For; Not for Dummies or Idiots; Real Expertise, Real Advice.

Step 4—Finalize the Concept and Refine

"Like Having Coffee with an Expert."

STEP 4 FINALIZE THE CONCEPT AND REFINE

The final stage involves nailing down the concept and direction you will use, then doing some final refining and testing. This is the point to start getting feedback from existing customers or others you trust about whether the message is working.

When we went through this exercise for the guide series, we ended up choosing "Like Having Coffee Expert." It was the one phrase that we felt brought the authenticity and approachability of the guide series to life through a recognizable moment: sharing a cup of coffee with a smart colleague or mentor.

It was a human way to describe the tone we wanted to achieve with the series and a perfect reminder of what our brand stands for: authoritative without being arrogant and useful without being obvious.

CHAPTER SUMMARY
KEY TAKEAWAYS:

- Positioning is the art of differentiating yourself in the mind of the consumer.

- Good marketing messages are tangible, clear, relevant, original, and elegant.

- Create your own tagline by starting with a list of relevant words and phrases.

CHAPTER 5

How to Build a Brand

In the early 1980s, the Pepsi Challenge asked consumers to do a blind taste test between Coke and Pepsi.

To everyone's surprise, many Coke drinkers chose Pepsi. The campaign gave Pepsi an immediate boost while sending Coca-Cola into a panic that led to the biggest flop in its history, launching "New Coke"—and then backtracking to reintroduce "Coca-Cola Classic."

While you might know this legendary business story, you may not have heard this follow up detail: *most of the people who participated in the taste test went right back to drinking Coke.*

Why? For Coke drinkers, the brand was such an ingrained part of their identity that even when confronted with the experiment's results, they could not imagine switching to Pepsi or describing themselves as a Pepsi drinker.

A brand can be a powerful force. So powerful it can drive people to ignore their own taste buds. My favorite definition of a brand comes from the American Marketing Association (AMA):

> A brand is a name, term, design, symbol, or any other feature that identifies one seller's goods or services as distinct from those of other sellers.

Your business needs a strong brand because having one allows you to charge more than your competitors and inspire greater loyalty from your customers. This chapter will teach you how to build one, or strengthen the one you already have.

> You can build a brand around any name. But the right name will make your life much easier.

5.1 | The Eight Types of Brand Names (and How to Use Them)

Picking the right brand name can be a combination of art and science, but it can feel like a lot of pressure.

How can you tell if you have the right name? If you are struggling with what to name your business or how to leverage the name you currently have, chances are you haven't uncovered the best way to talk about it. Knowing what type of name you have can help. Here's a chart that describes eight common types:

BRAND NAME TYPE	WHAT IS IT?	EXAMPLES	WHY IT WORKS
Familial	Based on the name of the founder(s)	Ben & Jerry's, Bosch, McDonald's, Kellogg's	Personal, authentic, historic
Logical*	Based on the product or service you sell	Next Day Blinds, Burger King, BMW, Non-Obvious	Clear, descriptive, easy to understand
Benefit-Focused	Based on a sales benefit or product attribute	Best Buy, Payless, Rubbermaid	Sales-oriented, incorporates a pitch, actionable
Geographic	Based on your heritage or where you come from	Norwegian Cruises, North Face, Credit Suisse, Washington Post	Historic, authentic, memorable
Thematic	Based on a recognizable word, phrase, or concept	Tide, Glad, Peloton, New Balance	Familiar, ownable, simple

Mashup	Based on a combination of words or ideas	Clearasil, Ideapress, Facebook, Duracell	Unique, subconsciously familiar
Random	Based on a random but usually recognized word	Apple, Shell, Blackberry, Dodge, Domino's, Sharp	Familiar, unexpected, potentially ownable
Domain	Based on a memorable URL you can register	www.yahoo.com	Memorable, actionable

__Note:__ Most of the widely known acronyms for business names, such as BBC or IBM, usually fit into this category if you consider what the acronyms stand for.

5.2	# The Importance of Brand Consistency

I have spent hundreds of hours of my life obsessing over colors, icons, and fonts to portray brands. Of course, that's probably because it was usually my job to help create them. At a large brand, this kind of obsession translates into how they communicate a uniform message and style. Here is an example from the Non-Obvious brand guidelines on logo usage.

As you can see from the examples shown, there are visual guidelines for how our logo can and cannot be used. The logo should not be distorted or placed upon a dark background. It also cannot be used on merchandise without permission. Ultimately, the guidelines exist to help make sure you tell a cohesive brand story.

| Good branding is all about consistency.

As you think about building your own brand, this probably seems like overkill. Even though you probably don't need so many specifications (especially if you're usually the only one using the brand), you should take away this one lesson...

Being consistent in branding means communicating one unified identity and message through the presentation of your products and services. However, this doesn't mean that everything always needs to look the same or be completely inflexible.

CASE STUDY: TRADER JOE'S BRAND

Trader Joe's has a well-recognized brand—despite the fact that they often use culturally adapted versions for some products. Italian private-label pasta products, for example, are promoted under a brand called *Trader Giotto's*. Chunky salsa is from *Trader Jose's*, and Pad Thai noodles come from *Trader Ming's*

A variety of Trader Joe's brand packaging

Even while changing the name of the brand, Trader Joe's is maintaining consistency in how it is presented to customers through the style of the packaging and the fact that the products are available only in their clearly branded grocery stores. For Trader Joe's, the variations help bring the brand personality of playfulness to life. It is also a refreshing example of why style guides do not have to feel overly corporate or lack personality in order to work.

5.3 Defining Your Brand—How to Set Non-Obsessive Guidelines

Brand consistency doesn't just happen.

While you probably don't need a 70-page guide, you do need to create an outline to address some basic questions and help you (and anyone else using your brand) to maintain consistency:

→ **Visual:** Should the logo always be presented in its entirety, or can components be used separately?

→ **Placement:** Does your logo need to appear in a certain location or a certain format?

→ **Pairing:** Is there a tagline that must be presented along with the logo? If so, how should that look? Can they ever be separated?

→ **Backgrounds:** Can your logo be placed against any color background? Do you have a "reverse logo," with a white or light-colored version that can be used against a black background?

Ideapress Publishing's logo and reverse logo

➔ **Sizing:** Is there a minimum size that your logo can be printed or a certain amount of space that must be allowed around it?

➔ **Fonts:** What fonts can be used alongside the logo or to write your brand name? Do you have an official font?

**CHAPTER SUMMARY
KEY TAKEAWAYS:**

- A brand is a way to identify your products and services as distinct from the competition.

- The most important thing to remember when trying to build a brand is to be consistent.

- There are eight types of brand names: familial, logical, benefit-focused, geographic, thematic, mashup, random, and domain.

CHAPTER 6

How to Tell Your Story

Have you ever watched the end of a Jackie Chan film? They are all mostly the same.

Before the final credits scroll, they show a compilation of outtakes. As you watch him trying (and sometimes failing) to do the crazy stunts he does on camera, you appreciate the talent it took to jump through a half-open window at full speed or slide down the outside of a skyscraper.

The outtakes show how hard he works to get all his stunts exactly right. He was even rumored to have shot one short scene more than 2,900 times just to get it perfect!

Chan and his producers expertly do the same thing that your math teacher always told you to do back in grade school: show your work.

Storytelling lets you take people behind the scenes to inspire more appreciation for your final product.

When you use storytelling for marketing purposes, it creates a reason for people to believe in what you do and adds context to their understanding of why you are different. One way to do this is by providing a backstory, including the history behind your company and why it exists today.

6.1	How to Tell Your Backstory

A backstory is not a timeline of accomplishments or a recital of boring details that often can be found on a company website. I once read the "story" of a regional bank that was basically a list of every time it acquired a smaller bank or moved its headquarters in the course of 80 years.

That is not a story.

A backstory, when done properly, is something more meaningful. It has real characters and a believable tale of how a business had to evolve and overcome challenges in order to become successful.

A good backstory should answer all of these questions:

1. **Characters:** Who are the people in the story, and why should we care about them?

2. **Challenge:** What is the key question or need that they address?

3. **Vision:** What was the unique idea or mission they set out to achieve?

4. **Conflict:** Who or what stands in the way of their success?

5. **Triumph:** How do the characters overcome this conflict?

These are the building blocks of all effective stories, whether it is about the founding of your company or a screenplay for a Hollywood film.

There are five typical backstories that you can consider using to tell the backstory of your business:

1. THE PASSIONATE ENTHUSIAST

A driven individual or group builds on a personal passion or interest to create a successful business.

A perfect example is The Last Bookstore in Los Angeles, founded by Josh Spencer. In 2005, he worked to create a massive retail space that was "a mix of Victorian drawing room, sci-fi spectacle and artist loft bohemianism." Today it is one of the largest independent bookstores in the world.

CASE STUDY: BIRA BEER

It took two years for Bira 91 to become one of India's most popular beer brands.

When creating the company, Indian entrepreneur Ankur Jain knew the popularity and acceptance of microbreweries that he had encountered when living in Brooklyn, New York, did not exist in India.

So he created a microbrewery of his own.

In 2015, Bira 91 launched with a Belgian-style white ale. Today the beer is created using locally sourced wheat and aromatic coriander from Indian farms. Embracing his heritage as an Indian, Jain believes that his creation can succeed through the force of his personality and the authenticity of the story he tells.

His is one of a Passionate Enthusiast.

2. THE INSPIRED INVENTOR

A tireless inventor designs something new and different by not giving up on his or her vision.

One recognizable example is James Dyson and how he made more than 2,000 prototype designs of his bagless vacuum cleaner (at a time when all other vacuums had bags). His innovation eventually led to the creation of the Dyson company, which now invents and sells much more than just vacuum cleaners.

STORY: SOUTHWEST AIRLINES

Two men walk into a bar and start an airline.

That's the short version of Southwest Airlines' founding story. The two men were Rollin King, a pilot, and Herb Kelleher, a lawyer. The conversation, later commemorated with a plaque at Southwest headquarters, supposedly went like this:

"Herb, let's start an airline."

"Rollin, you're crazy. Let's do it!"

They drew their business vision on a cocktail napkin: Create an airline that offered direct flights multiple times a day between three cities in Texas: Dallas, Houston, and San Antonio.

This initial clarity was crucial to ensuring that everyone in the company was aligned with their vision from the start. Southwest would eventually become the most profitable airline in the world. Shortly before he died, King admitted that the story about the napkin might not have been entirely accurate, but it was a "hell of a good story." By that point, it had become part of the company's history.

3. THE SMART LISTENER

An entrepreneur creates a customer-centric company after deeply listening to customers, partners, or others.

Stacy's Pita Chips, for example, is a company founded in response to consumers who continually told sandwich cart owner Stacy Madison that they loved her pita chips and that she should start a business just making and selling those. So she did—and eventually sold it to PepsiCo.

4. THE LIKEABLE HERO

A dedicated individual launches a business that makes the world better or solves an urgent human problem.

Entrepreneur Blake Mycoskie, who founded Toms Shoes with the mission of donating millions of shoes to kids in need, exemplifies this type of backstory.

5. THE LITTLE GUY VS. THE BIG GUY

An underdog company takes on a seemingly unbeatable, established adversary.

Samples of companies with this story include Under Armour (vs. Nike) and Lyft (vs. Uber).

If you think about the story of Southwest Airlines, it has interesting elements of multiple backstories. The founders were *Inspired Inventors*, they were *Smart Listeners*, and when they started, they were the *Little Guy vs. the Big Guy* in the aviation industry.

VISIT ONLINE RESOURCES FOR:
A guide to using the backstory models in this chapter from
Personality Not Included.

Your business can also use these different story types to tell different parts of your backstory. You don't have to fit neatly into one category. Instead, the aim of these models is to give you a framework and idea for how to craft your story in a way that gives people a reason to believe in your business.

6.2	**How to Use Personality to Tell Your Story**

Personality is the spark that brings your backstory to life and helps you make a deeper connection with your current and prospective customers.

> Your personality is the unique, authentic, and talkable soul of your brand that inspires connection.

Here are five tips for how to bring your personality into the marketing for your business.

TIP 1   STAND FOR SOMETHING

In 2005, a Wisconsin dentist named Dr. Chris Kammer started offering to buy his patients' leftover Halloween candy for $1 per pound and send it to U.S. military forces overseas. The idea started a movement with thousands of dentists eventually participating, and the publicity helped Kammer attract plenty of new patients.

TIP 2   HAVE A SENSE OF HUMOR

Law firms don't tend to be funny, but at the Valorem Law Group in Chicago, humor and wit are essential to communicating who its ideal clients are and are not. For example, here is the firm's unusual disclaimer:

> *We can relate to people, which means we don't do tax law. Nothing in the site refers to or mentions tax law. If you have a tax question, you're in the wrong place. Find a tax lawyer. Preferably one with a personality. Again, don't hold your breath.*

If a law firm can have this much fun and speak this plainly in its own disclaimer, you can imagine what kind of authentic experience their clients might have working with them.

TIP 3   CREATE AN IMMERSIVE EXPERIENCE

Steve Busti lives in Austin, Texas, a quirky city that demands visitors and residents alike to "Keep Austin Weird." Embracing this personality, Busti launched a *Museum of the Weird* and filled it with unusual items from around the world. In the process, he created an experience that felt just weird enough to fit right in with Austin's culture.

TIP 4   ANSWER THE WHY

Having a personality means being willing to bend or even break the rules when no one can explain them. Think about the rules in your business. Are they there for a reason that you can explain if someone asks? If not, get rid of them!

TIP 5   USE YOUR PERSONALITY MOMENTS

A personality moment is a customer interaction where you can create a connection. This can be the "unboxing" moment when a customer unwraps a product or the first time they walk into your store. Your brand comes to life in small moments like this, especially when you take the time to think about how to inject more personality into them.

CHAPTER SUMMARY
KEY TAKEAWAYS:

- Build trust by taking people behind the scenes and showing your work.

- Your personality is the spark that brings your company's backstory to life.

- There are five backstory models: the Passionate Enthusiast, the Inspired Inventor, the Smart Listener, the Likeable Hero, and the Little Guy vs. the Big Guy.

CHAPTER 7

How to Inspire Word of Mouth

I am far more annoyed by the inconvenience of getting a haircut than I should be. I get frustrated at the slow ritual of taking a number, waiting for my turn, and even sitting in the chair for the haircut itself. It all just seems like a waste of time.

Of course, I could make an appointment at a salon, but I don't really have enough hair left on my head to justify that expense. Instead, I do what most guys I know do: show up at the barbershop, hope there's not a crowd, and wait.

One day, a friend told me about Andy's Barber Shop, a local place that always has at least eight barbers working at a time. After trying it one time, the shop became my favorite because it was faster.

The way I found that barbershop was the same way that I discovered and hired a graphic designer, a music teacher, a landscape architect, and a lawyer. They all came through personal referrals. This is what most of us call *word of mouth*, and it has always been the most effective form of marketing.

There is no marketing as good as getting your customers to recommend you. Making it happen, though, takes more than providing a great product or service.

7.1 Why Customer Satisfaction Doesn't Matter

It is common to have a satisfying experience with a product or service and promptly forget about it. The problem is not the experience; it's that we don't always have a *reason* to share it.

> A good experience alone isn't enough to get people talking.

Most people are busy, and promoting your product, service or cause will never be high on their list of priorities. Part of the reason is that delivering what they expect from you is hardly cause for celebration. Do you go out of your way to rave about your doctor's appointment every time they deliver the care you expected? Do you review every book you read on Amazon? Of course, the answer is no.

What does it take to get reluctant and busy customers talking and referring?

7.2	**The UAT Filter**

Persuading people to share positive experiences and referrals comes down to three basic qualities: being unique, authentic, and talkable. I call this the UAT filter—a way to bring together the elements of an experience that people will love and be more likely to share.

How can you use this concept to better prepare your business for generating unstoppable word-of-mouth marketing? To answer that question, let's take a deeper look at each element of the UAT filter.

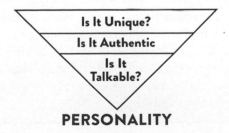

| 7.3 | **How to Be More Unique** |

For years, a regional auto shop called Oil Can Henry's differentiated itself as the most honest mechanic in town. They did it by letting customers watch a mechanic working under their car on a live video feed throughout the service. By letting customers stay with their cars, they reinforced trust that they were not doing anything sneaky.

Being unique is all about doing something no one else does. Like letting your customers watch while you service their car.

CASE STUDY:
TAKING SELFIES AT AZIZ ANSARI'S SHOW

If you attend a live stand-up comedy performance by actor Aziz Ansari, you'll see him start with an unusual bit. He gives everyone in the audience permission to pull out their phones and take a photo. He even strikes a few poses before telling the audience to share their photos on social media (great word-of-mouth marketing!)—and then put their phones away and enjoy the rest of the show. At a theater show where the most basic rule is "no photos and no recording," Ansari takes that rule and adds a twist. It makes a unique opening and generates lots of word of mouth on social media.

7.4   How to Be More Authentic

We are surrounded by examples of fake authenticity. We can buy "hand-carved" sandwich meats that are processed in factories and supposedly "artisan" Italian luggage manufactured in Asia. Authenticity may have become a common business buzzword, but actually finding it in reality is getting harder and harder.

> Authenticity starts with a believable heritage.

Kikkoman, a Japanese company that makes soy sauce, produced a short documentary about the 400-year-old history of their brand. Titled *Make Haste Slowly*, it is authentic, historic, and tells the powerful story of how the brand came to the United States.[4] I have shared their example many times on stage during keynote presentations—and in the process generated word-of-mouth marketing for a product most people otherwise wouldn't think much about.

And now I buy only Kikkoman soy sauce.

VISIT ONLINE RESOURCES FOR:
A link to watch the Kikkoman documentary film *Make Haste Slowly*.

This type of authenticity comes from your backstory, which we talked about in Chapter 6. When you can share your story authentically, it demonstrates that you have real people behind your business and helps to build trust.

| 7.5 | **How to Be More Talkable** |

In *The Power of Moments*, authors and brothers Chip and Dan Heath tell the story of the Magic Castle Hotel in Los Angeles, which routinely outranks top-tier properties such as the Four Seasons. The most popular feature there is a cherry-red phone near the pool. It's called the Popsicle Hotline and is used to order frozen treats, delivered poolside on a silver tray by a staffer wearing white gloves—all for free.

That is more than a good experience. It is so unusual and memorable that guests can't help wanting to share it, as hundreds of people have in rave reviews online.

How can you empower the people who love your product or service to rave about it to others? You might do it by sharing products, giving them an exclusive experience, or engaging them online or in person and asking for their advice on what you could do better.

7.6 How to Inspire Your Employees, Teammates, and Vendors to Be Ambassadors

Your employees could be your greatest drivers of positive buzz and word of mouth, but they won't always do so without a little nudge.

Though many of them might be willing to help you promote your business, it can be hard to know how to engage them. The first step is to better understand how they feel about your business— and what you might do to improve.

> No one will recommend someone or something that they don't believe in.

Here are a few tips that can help you better engage your employees and make it more likely they will help generate positive word of mouth for your business, too.

TIP 1 LEAD BY EXAMPLE

If your team doesn't see you promoting the business openly and consistently, why would they be invested in doing it? The best way to encourage employees to promote a brand at every turn is by leaders setting the example and doing it themselves.

TIP 2 ASK THEM HOW YOU CAN BE BETTER

Chances are your team has some ideas for how to improve what you do or even to grow your business. Listening to them and giving them a chance to develop ideas on their own not only demonstrates you care about their opinion but also has the added possibility that if you agree to their idea, they might be excited to help implement it.

TIP 3 ENCOURAGE THEM TO BE HUMAN

Do you rush your people through social interactions or try to focus on productivity at all costs? Conversations lead to word of mouth, so make it a priority for the people who work for you to take time to speak to your customers. Let them be human and they will have more of a chance to talk about your business.

TIP 4   SHARE THE SUCCESS

When employees help promote your business and it leads to more sales or more clients, find a way to help them share in the reward—through bonuses, celebrations, or awards. When a team feels like the windfall from a win is good for everyone, they will try harder to help you win more often.

TIP 5   ENCOURAGE TRANSPARENCY

Nothing will damage your credibility more than the perception that you are paying people to say nice things about your business. To avoid this perception, set some simple guidelines:

1. **Transparency:** Always be upfront about your business affiliation.

2. **Off-limit topics:** Forbid talking about other employees or sharing trade secrets.

3. **Acceptable voice:** Don't be rude, and choose to converse with kindness and humility.

**CHAPTER SUMMARY
KEY TAKEAWAYS:**

- The most effective form of marketing has always been and continues to be word of mouth.

- Satisfied customers may not talk about your business. Delighted customers often will.

- The three keys to driving word of mouth are being unique, authentic, and talkable.

PART TWO

Execution

Chapter 8

How to Create a Marketing Plan

On February 4, 2017, moments after the Atlanta Falcons suffered a heartbreaking overtime loss in Super Bowl 51, a mattress brand named Purple tweeted out a video featuring a dejected fan wearing a red Falcon's jersey stumbling to his bed with tears in his eyes. The accompanying message said:—*"What a comeback! Hope you Atlanta fans have a comfy place to cry..."*

The personality and timeliness injected into that video was nothing new for Purple. The brand has relied on videos and clever marketing to make a name for itself in the competitive sleep industry since they first launched nearly three years earlier on Kickstarter.

One of the ways they bring their brand to life is through a range of interesting brand characters. One video uses an actress playing Goldilocks and trying an "egg test" to illustrate how Purple mattresses have just the right amount of support for your sleep (not too hard and not too soft).

The 'Goldilocks' character from Purple advertising

Another video featured sumo wrestlers on the bed to demonstrate the strength of the mattress. The videos have racked up more than 500 million views and have helped propel the company to quick success and a merger valued at nearly $1 billion in 2017.[5]

VISIT ONLINE RESOURCES FOR:
A link to watch a few of the Purple marketing videos online.

This sequence of marketing efforts with multiple characters is a perfect example of how marketing is meant to work. Each one tells a distinct but related story about why a customer should consider you and they all work together.

8.1   The Art of Campaign Thinking

When it comes to bringing your marketing to life, a *marketing campaign* is a series of activities that help you to achieve a specific marketing objective. The more specific you can be about the objective, the easier it will be to measure and track whether it works.

Here are a few possible objectives for a marketing campaign:

→   Acquiring new customers or generating new leads

→   Increasing sales from existing customers

→   Launching a new product, service, or location

→   Announcing a new partnership or benefit

→   Promoting an award, honor, or other big news

Consider the example of Purple—they had an initial Kickstarter campaign to launch their company. They used Goldilocks as a way to define their competitive difference. The sumo campaign was designed to address the question of the durability and strength of the mattress. Each was a different marketing campaign.

<table>
<tr><td>**8.2**</td><td>

How to Simplify Your Marketing Plan

</td></tr>
</table>

Before planning any campaign, you'll need to create a clear marketing plan. To do this, let's review a one-page marketing plan template that outlines all the choices you need to make and information you need to define in order to build your own plan.

THE **NON-OBVIOUS 1 PAGE** MARKETING PLAN (DIRECTIONS)

The Message:
What will we say and how will we say it?

The Customer Persona:
Who are we trying to reach and what do they believe?

The Action or Belief:
What do we want our audience to do or say or believe as a result of our efforts?

The Destinations:
Where are we sending them to further engage with us?

The Drivers:
What channels and tactics will we use to reach them?

The Intended Result:
What do we hope to achieve and what tangible result will we look for to know if our efforts worked?

NON OBVIOUS GUIDE

VISIT ONLINE RESOURCES FOR:
A downloadable PDF of the 1-Page Marketing Plan.

The elements of this plan are topics that will be covered throughout the rest of the chapters of this book. Some, like positioning and consumer personas, are topics we have already covered. The point of this template is to bring everything together, but we haven't yet covered everything you'll see listed there.

The aim of this chapter, therefore, is to give you an overview of the plan, but you don't need to fill it out entirely quite yet. For now, let's just start by reviewing all the components.

8.3 The Elements of a Marketing Campaign Plan

The Non-Obvious Marketing Campaign Plan template introduced in this chapter contains six sections:

1. **The message:** What will we say, and how will we say it?

2. **The customer persona:** Who are we trying to reach, and what do they already believe?

3. **The action or belief:** What do we want our audience to do, say, or believe as a result of our efforts?

4. **The destinations:** Where are we trying to send them to further engage with us?

5. **The drivers:** What channels and tactics will we use to reach them?

6. **The intended results:** What do we hope to achieve, and what measurable goal are we working toward?

THE MESSAGE

Your main marketing message should align with your overall brand positioning and emphasize what sets you apart. In Chapter 4, we talked about how to create a tagline for your business. A tagline defines your business overall, while a campaign message is usually created for a specific objective or situation.

To see how your messaging might shift depending on your objectives, here are a few examples of campaign messages, along with a description of what the campaign is for.

BRAND	CAMPAIGN MESSAGE	WHAT IS IT FOR?
Heineken	"Now You Can"	New campaign introducing the Heineken 0.0 product—a non-alcoholic beer.
Rimowa Luggage	"No One Builds A Legacy By Standing Still"	Message for a new campaign featuring several celebrity spokespeople.
Taco Bell	"Feed The Beat"	Taco Bell's music program, which has helped support more than 1,500 artists/bands.

THE CUSTOMER PERSONA

In Chapter 3, you learned how to create a customer persona, a way to describe your customer that makes it clear what they would be most interested in so that your marketing campaign can be sure to address it. Here are a few examples along with the type of business that might use this persona:

→ A safe driver who thinks all car insurance is the same and hates paperwork (car insurance agent)

→ A thrill seeker who wants a local vacation between vacations (local zipline adventure park)

→ A busy professional reluctant to take time to care for herself (massage parlor)

THE ACTION OR BELIEF

Often described as the call to action, this is a short description of what you want your target audience to do after seeing your marketing communications.

Do you want them to fill out an online form, visit your website, watch your videos, or come to your store in person? Here are a few good examples of campaign calls to action from brands you might recognize:

→ "See What's Next. Watch Anywhere. Cancel Anytime. Join Free for a Month." (Netflix)

→ "Choose Independent. Choose Firefox. Free Download." (Firefox)

→ "Truth. It Comes at a Cost. Subscribe Now."
(*New York Times*)

THE DESTINATION

A destination is the digital or physical property where you direct your audience in a campaign to learn more about your products or services or to consume your content. You could send them to their local retailer if you're selling a product online, or you might send them to your social media profile page to participate in a sweepstakes or contest.

THE DRIVERS

How will you get people to visit or engage with your destinations? This is what drivers do. Examples include paid advertising, media, and content marketing to help people discover your destinations.

THE INTENDED RESULTS

In this part of the template, you want to define a measurable goal. In Chapter 18, we will discuss the difference between goals that can be measured and goals that can't. In that chapter, you will also learn how to write a good goal statement.

8.4   Why You Need Integration

I remember when I was leading the marketing efforts for a large brand of orange juice, and we had a meeting with representatives from each of its agencies. The goal was to make sure that our plan was integrated because the campaign was complex. *Twelve different groups were in attendance.*

Of course, you are probably not working with a dozen agencies simultaneously, so integration should be easy for you, right? Maybe not.

The following story is an example of how a lack of integration can cause problems for any size business.

STORY: PEACH SEASON IS OVER

Imagine you are driving along the highway, and you see a sign promoting a farmer's market that has fresh peaches. You love peaches, so you decide to stop. But the only fruit you see is pears.

"Sorry," the owner tells you, "but peach season is over. We just haven't updated the sign yet."

It turns out that peaches grow in the summer, and pears come in the autumn. But you didn't know that, and the farm didn't change the sign, so you had a negative experience. This is what a lack of alignment creates: a disjointed customer experience and disappointment.

When you think about marketing, this challenge of integration is always present.

If you are running keyword ads on Google promoting your email newsletter, for example, are you sending users to your home page where the signup form is hard to find? Do the look and feel of your print ad match the logo and sign hanging above your physical store?

The best marketing campaigns, like the best brands, are always integrated.

**CHAPTER SUMMARY
KEY TAKEAWAYS:**

- Simplicity is key when putting together a marketing strategy.

- The best marketing campaigns have specific objectives and measurable business goals.

- The six elements of a marketing plan include the message, the customer persona, the action or belief, the destinations, the drivers, and the intended results.

Chapter 9

How to Create a Kick-Ass Website

Web developers joke that there are only two types of websites: those that have just been launched and those that are badly in need of a redesign.

For many organizations, launching a website is a mixed blessing. The moment when it goes live feels great. But very soon after, we discover how much effort it takes to keep the site up to date and useful. Is it even worth it?

If you're not in an online business, it's easy to think your site isn't so important. Thinking that would be a mistake.

Your website matters because prospective customers will often visit it before working with you.

9.1   The Four Reasons People Visit Your Website

Why are people visiting your website? Usually it is for one of four reasons:

1. **Validation:** Once aware of a service or product, prospective customers often end up on your website to validate what they have heard about you.

2. **Research:** Some site visitors seek specific information such as your physical address or want to see some examples of your experience and past work.

3. **Connection:** Some customers visit your site intending to connect with you via phone or email.

4. **Conversion:** Some users will visit ready to make a purchase or book an appointment or join your list.

If you can optimize your online experience to help your visitors get what they seek, you can make it more likely they will ultimately do business with you. To do this, your first and most important challenge is to demonstrate that you and your business are trustworthy.

9.2 The Five Elements of a Trustworthy Website

When eBay launched more than two decades ago, people were generally afraid of putting any personal information online and particularly skeptical of buying something from a stranger.

For the platform to succeed, the company had to create their own metric for trust—which they did with their star rating system. In solving this challenge, eBay was one of the first companies to create a form of virtual trust through which people could make transactions without any face-to-face contact.

Here are five ways for you to use this same principle to build virtual and real-life trust through the experience you offer on your website:

1. **Update your design**. Are you still using the same website design from 2015? When you have an outdated or poorly designed website, you are sending a negative signal to the world about your business? Investing in a professionally designed website helps build trust in your brand online. With the number of high-quality do-it-yourself tools available today, there is no excuse for a bad website anymore.

2. **Humanize your voice.** The voice you use on your site is critical, from the tone of the writing to the choice of language. Buzzwords create boredom, and corporate language creates distrust. To use more human language, read your website copy out loud. If it sounds like something you would say in a conversation, then keep it. If not, change it!

3. **Make it usable.** Is your information organized in a logical way? Is the most important information highly prominent and easily scanned? Usability means your customers can easily accomplish their goals on your site.

4. **Integrate social proof.** Endorsements from media or influencers can help inspire trust in your business. This might be a news article or a customer quote. For more on this topic, read Chapter 16.

5. **Tell your story.** Are your story and content tied to the real people behind your organization? Do you show your team on your site? Your "About Us" page is likely to be one of the most frequently visited spots on your site, so the more human and visual you can make it, the better.

9.3   How to Fix Your Website Quickly

Does your website suck?

This may not be an easy question to answer because most of us don't know how to evaluate our own website objectively. This is not a question of your background color or your images. Can people find the information they want? Are you effectively addressing the four reasons they might be visiting your site?

To help evaluate your site, download the assessment tool below that includes key questions and criteria.

If you conducted the website audit, how did you do? Don't worry if you ended up with a list of issues to address; that is common.

At this point, you may be worried that you lack the technical skills to fix those problems. The good news is that you can implement several changes to improve your site quickly—and some don't require much technical expertise at all.

VISIT ONLINE RESOURCES FOR:
A downloadable audit template that will help evaluate your site and uncover problems that need fixing.

TIP 1   FOCUS ON THE HOME PAGE

The home page of your site is the gateway to your business and makes the first impression. Does it introduce what you do well? Is it clear what the visitor should do next? While a full redesign may be too much work, redoing your home page can be a high impact first step in giving people a positive experience on your site and encouraging them to engage with you further.

TIP 2   ANNOUNCE A REDESIGN

The only thing worse than a bad website is one that seems as if it will be bad forever. Put a note on your home page promising that your redesign is coming soon. The side benefit is that once you publicly commit to improving the site, you're much more likely to follow through and get it done.

TIP 3   USE EMBEDDABLE CONTENT

When you use other platforms such as YouTube or SlideShare to create content, you can embed the content on your website easily by cutting and pasting some programming code. Using an existing presentation or video can be a quick way to add information to your site without having to create new pages or write new content.

TIP 4   UPDATE YOUR DATES

A telltale sign of a neglected website is a lonely copyright message at the bottom of the page revealing the year you last updated it. If your copyright message is from 2018 or earlier, update it immediately. Use a range instead, such as "Copyright 2010-2019," or remove the date altogether.

9.4	Going Responsive: Why You Need a Mobile-Friendly Site

According to research firm Zenith Media, mobile devices already account for 79 percent of all Internet traffic and that number will continue to grow.[6] Have you tested what your site looks like on a smaller screen?

> The best websites are responsive, which means they adjust dynamically to the size of any screen.

It is hard to retrofit a website to be responsive if it hasn't been built that way intentionally. If that is the case with your site, a complete redesign may be in order.

VISIT ONLINE RESOURCES FOR:
Advice on website design tools and platforms to consider.

If you're not sure look at your site on a mobile phone. or a tablet. If the content automatically adjusts to fit the screen, your site is responsive.

**CHAPTER SUMMARY
KEY TAKEAWAYS:**

- Anyone considering working with you or buying from you will probably visit your website.

- The four reasons people visit your website are for validation, research, connection, or conversion.

- Conduct a site audit to test if you are delivering the experience your customers want.

Chapter 10

How to Use
Social Media

In 2004, I started writing a blog. It was a few months before Facebook officially launched. YouTube, Twitter, and Instagram had not yet appeared. Over the next five years, everything changed.

More platforms emerged, and brands started investing lots of resources into figuring out how to use social media effectively. At the time I was working at what would later become one of the world's biggest team of social media experts.

My role involved leading engagements for Ford, Intel, Johnson & Johnson, and a handful of other big brands. I was paid to specialize in social media and sell it as a tool that every brand should use. As a result, I approached every problem assuming social media was the solution.

I had become a "social media evangelist" by accident. I'm not proud of it.

10.1	**Why No One Likes an Evangelist**

Most people who consider themselves evangelists share a singular and unchangeable worldview. They believe that everyone should love the same products, services, beliefs, or ideas that they love. They are closed-minded, one-directional, and exhausting to interact with.

> Evangelists don't see the world as it is. They see it as a place that would be better if everyone agreed with them.

The day I realized I was an evangelist, I started to change my perspective. I began to look at the good and the bad of social media. I stopped assuming that everyone needed to use it and started thinking about when it worked and when it failed.

Along the way, I discovered a few extremely common pieces of terrible advice that are frequently offered by people who don't know any better.

10.2	**The Biggest Myths About Social Media Marketing**

If you are going to use social media effectively, it helps to start by knowing what advice to ignore. Here are three of the worst social media "rules" that you should ignore.

MYTH 1 FOCUS ON THE COMMENTS

The comments on a YouTube video are usually a mix of stupidity, juvenile observations, racism/sexism, and spam. Thanks to anonymous online commenting, many people take little responsibility for what they say. Most Internet consumers already filter them out. There is only one good response to comments like those: ignore them.

MYTH 2 CUSTOMERS PREFER CONVERSATIONS

Imagine you're trying to book a flight to see family in Barcelona, withdraw cash from an ATM, or find a movie showtime. Do you really want to have a *conversation* about any of these things? Of course not. Sometimes we just want to get what we need and be on our way.

MYTH 3   IT'S ALL ABOUT CREATING CONTENT

Creating content can be a valuable way to attract eyeballs, but discerning what content will drive business results is not always easy. What if you don't have the skills or expertise? In Chapter 11, we will focus on using what you do have to build a smart Content Marketing strategy.

10.3	The Five Guiding Principles of Social Media

PRINCIPLE 1   BE TRANSPARENT

Conversations are public on social media, so it's good practice to share your business name and affiliations. It helps make sure no one feels that you are hiding something or being dishonest.

PRINCIPLE 2   HAVE A POINT OF VIEW

Rather than only sharing content from others, find a way to create or share content that uses your unique point of view to add an opinion or insight. People respond to those who have something interesting to say.

PRINCIPLE 3   USE A HUMAN VOICE

People expect to hear a real voice on social media, not a corporate drone. It is important to relate to people the same way as if you meet them in person.

PRINCIPLE 4   MAKE IT VISUAL

Content featuring images or video tends to get more attention. If you can create multimedia content, even if it's simple, it can help you increase your engagement dramatically.

PRINCIPLE 5   THINK BEFORE SHARING

Social media can make it particularly tempting to react with emotion in real-time. That's not the case. There is always time to calm down, consider what you post, and say what you mean. It's much better than regretting what you shared and having to backtrack.

VISIT ONLINE RESOURCES FOR:
A downloadable PDF with these five guiding principles that you can share with your team.

10.4 How to Pick Which Platforms to Use

The more platforms you create profiles for, the more content you will need to manage and maintain. Rather than trying to be everywhere at once, concentrate your efforts on the platforms that best serve your business goals.

> You don't need to be active on every social media platform.

How do you decide which platforms to use? The key point in the advice above is the word "active." There are four strategies that you can use with social media platforms, and not all of them require you to be active all the time. Let's review each of them.

STRATEGY 1   DEMONSTRATE YOUR PERSONALITY

Bring your brand to life through photos, videos, quotes, anecdotes, and stories.

STRATEGY 2   SHARE YOUR EXPERTISE

Use your knowledge to share content about the topic or industry of your experience.

STRATEGY 3   JOIN THE COMMUNITY

Be an active participant in a community of people with similar interests. Build your credibility by engaging and learning.

STRATEGY 4   CREATE A PLACEHOLDER

Claim a profile or custom URL and create a static page that invites people to connect with you elsewhere. It's a virtual sign that says the equivalent of "We've moved. Check out our new location!"

THE **NON-OBVIOUS 1 PAGE** SOCIAL MEDIA STRATEGY (DIRECTIONS)

Username: [Enter username here – the less characters the better!]

What username can you register consistently across most social media platforms? Pick something unique (and available)!

Strategy #1:	Strategy #2:	Strategy #3:	Strategy #4:
DEMONSTRATE PERSONALITY	**SHARE YOUR EXPERTISE**	**JOIN THE COMMUNITY**	**CREATE A PLACEHOLDER**
How To Use This Strategy:	**How To Use This Strategy:**	**How To Use This Strategy:**	**How To Use This Strategy:**
Bring the human side of your brand to life with photos of your team or office, personal images, quotes, anecdotes and other highly personal content designed to build connection with your audience and show an authentic side of your brand.	Use the knowledge you have about your industry or topic and share it freely online through creating content, participating in interviews, answering questions in forums and taking existing content and finding ways to distribute it widely.	Learn where your audience or people who have similar interests to you are conversing online and join the community as a willing participant who listens, learns, engages and finds ways to appropriately share useful + non-promotional thoughts or perspectives.	Claim your brand name to make sure that no one else takes it and create a placeholder profile that just shares some basic information and links back to your other platforms where you are more active and people can connect with you.
LIST OF PLATFORMS:	**LIST OF PLATFORMS:**	**LIST OF PLATFORMS:**	**LIST OF PLATFORMS:**
Which social media platforms will you use this strategy on?	Which social media platforms will you use this strategy on?	Which social media platforms will you use this strategy on?	Which social media platforms will you use this strategy on?

The 5 Guiding Principles Of Social Media:

Be Transparent / Have A Point Of View / Use A Human Voice / Make It Visual / Think Before Sharing

NON OBVIOUS GUIDE

VISIT ONLINE RESOURCES FOR:
A template to create your strategy for using social media platforms.

STORY: HOW I ABANDONED MY TWITTER ACCOUNT

When I launched my second book, *Likeonomics*, I created a Twitter account to promote it and started tweeting as if the book itself had a personality. It was a fun marketing campaign, but I ended it after less than a year because the book launch was over.

My main account on Twitter was @rohitbhargava, and the last thing I wanted to do was to maintain two accounts. But I also didn't want to erase the book's page because someone might search for me or the book on Twitter and expect to find it.

So I posted one last tweet (see below) and left the account online as a placeholder. You can use this same technique to claim a user name or page on social media and keep it only to send people where they will be able to engage with you.

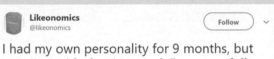

Likeonomics
@likeonomics

Follow ⌄

I had my own personality for 9 months, but now I've said what I wanted. For more, follow @rohitbhargava. Clearly he has more time than I do.

4:55 PM - 5 Mar 2013

10.5 Why Haters on Social Media Are a Good Thing

Haters—those who are disgruntled enough to actively talk about their dislike of you or your business—are easy to spot. They often find their way onto social media and sometimes their comments become highly visible thanks to search engines or third-party platforms that feature them.

> *Haters are not your problem. Ignoring them is.*
> —Jay Baer, author of Hug Your Haters

Though it may not seem like it, these haters can be a good thing. Here are a few reasons why.

REASON 1   HATERS EXPOSE VULNERABILITY

No business is perfect, and haters sometimes have valid points. It requires an open mind to focus on the substance of a complaint instead of reacting emotionally. If you can do this, your business can grow stronger because you can focus on the real issue that needs to be addressed.

REASON 2   HATERS CAN BE CONVERTED

The usual haters are not your lifelong enemies, but rather people who have had a single negative experience and felt compelled to share it. If you can resolve that experience, make up for it somehow, or help that person feel heard and respected, sometimes they can be transformed into your biggest advocate.

REASON 3   HATERS GENERATE ATTENTION

Though I do not believe that "any publicity is good publicity," any conversation about your business online can generate visibility. That attention can be a good thing. For example, one reviewer for my second book shared an angry review because there was an obvious, stupid typo in the book.

I immediately responded to apologize and told him I was extremely embarrassed. He replied and talked about how much he loved the book otherwise. He ended up becoming a major fan.

REASON 4 HATERS VALIDATE YOUR SOCIAL MEDIA EFFORTS

If you have used social media actively, the goodwill that you have built up with fans and followers can come in handy when haters appear. The people you have built a relationship with often will stick up for you against an unfair attack.

10.6 Do You Need to Hire a Social Media Consultant?

If you are feeling overwhelmed by social media, hiring a consultant can seem like a good choice. While many people claim to be experts in social media, there's more to it than gathering likes.

A good consultant won't blindly promise you X number of fans or Y number of impressions. Without knowing who those fans are or where those impressions are coming from, they offer only empty attention.

> Having lots of followers on social media doesn't matter if they don't care about you.

Would you welcome 10,000 new fans to your Facebook page who are uninterested in what you sell and located halfway around the world? Or would you rather have 100 highly qualified new fans who are likely to buy your products or services?

To determine whether you are working with a knowledgeable professional or a self-inflated "guru," here are a few questions to ask:

1. How long have you been working in social media?

2. Can you share an example of one organization you helped and how you did it?

3. What is the biggest mistake you have seen companies like ours make with social media?

4. What do you think we should do first?

5. How will I know whether our efforts are working?

6. What will you do to ensure our efforts are ethical?

7. What real business results should we expect?

Based on the answers they share, you can better evaluate whether their skills and expertise are right for your business.

CHAPTER SUMMARY
KEY TAKEAWAYS:

- Always be transparent, have a point of view, use a human voice, make it visual, and think before sharing.

- The four social media strategies are demonstrating your personality, sharing your expertise, joining the community, or creating a placeholder.

- Don't be afraid to engage haters with substance and dialogue to address their issues.

Chapter 11

How to Do Content Marketing

When I turned to the Internet for advice on buying a new grill, the first thing I learned was that I would need to choose between charcoal or gas.

I had no idea how to pick.

After a quick Google search, I discovered a short PDF with the simple title "How to Choose a Grill." I downloaded it and started learning all the pros and cons of the two options. The last page of the PDF was a checklist to fill out and take to my local dealer when I was ready to buy.

The following weekend, I brought my completed checklist into a local hardware store and the sales guy immediately led me to both types of grills made by Weber. It was a logical choice because the PDF I used was written and published by Weber.

I walked out of the store that day with a Weber grill (charcoal, by the way) because the company provided a great answer to my question of what type of grill I should buy right when I needed that advice.

Here's the Weber charcoal grill 1 ended up buying!

That is the power of content marketing.

11.1 Why Content Marketing Is So Popular

Imagine if the owner of a hardware store had written that PDF and contrasted Weber grills with another brand. I might have gone there and walked out with a different grill purchase.

Content marketing is a hot topic in the overall world of marketing, and the reason for its popularity is simple: it works.

> Imagine if your marketing was so valuable that people wanted to consume and willingly share it.

Great content answers customer questions and provides a tangible way to demonstrate your expertise.

The process is often described as *inbound marketing* because it focuses on using compelling content such as white papers, webinars, live chat sessions, and email newsletters to engage customers and answer their questions.

11.2 How to Find Topics People Care About

The success of any content marketing starts with a strong understanding of what people want to know. Here are four ways that you can find those topics:

1. **Frequently asked questions:** What are the most typical questions that your customers ask? This is a perfect place to start when deciding what content to create. Can you answer those questions in a way that reaches more people and helps you promote your business?

2. **Keywords + search phrases:** What sort of keywords or phrases might your customers use when searching for information related to your industry online? Taking time to search the web as a customer is an ideal way to understand what information they might be seeking.

3. **Surveys + audience polls:** The best way to find out what a group wants is to ask them, but who should you ask? There are a growing number of online survey tools to help you ask questions from your own audience or conduct open polls of people on social media.

4. **Media + competitor landscape:** Watch what your competitors are doing by searching for information from them as if you were a consumer. How could you learn from and improve on their efforts?

11.3 How to Create Content to Show Your Expertise

Whether you provide consultative services or sell retail products in a store, your expertise is a gold mine and content marketing can help you leverage it. Here are a few ideas for making this happen.

TIP 1 PROACTIVELY ANSWER QUESTIONS

People routinely post questions online and answering them generously can help you build more trust with your audience. This is the strategy often employed by B2B companies when they publish surveys, white papers, and other expert insights. They are sharing their wisdom to build trust with their audience and to be seen as credible experts worthy of attention and respect.

TIP 2 FOCUS ON "HOW TO" CONTENT

"How to" is a frequent search phrase, so it is good to create content for common activities that people are trying to learn. Many top yoga instructors, for example, post videos on YouTube showing how to do popular poses. That content can attract more students to come to their classes in person.

TIP 3 POSITION YOURSELF AS A COMPELLING GUEST

What media properties does your audience respect most? If there is an industry magazine that has a wide circulation, you should get to know the journalists who contribute there. If your audience listens to certain influencers on social media, you should be listening to them and trying to engage them as well. See Chapter 16 for more on this topic.

TIP 4 POLISH AN EVERGREEN "CONTENT BOMB"

A content bomb sits online until a relevant search helps someone find it. For example, early in my speaking career, I wrote an article titled "How to Moderate a Great Panel Discussion." It helped event planners to discover and consider me as a speaker or MC for their event and continues to drive traffic to my website even today.

11.4 What Are You Good At?

The prospect of starting a blog or creating your own content may sound daunting.

The biggest reason content marketing initiatives fail is because people try to do something they can't sustain and dislike doing. Imagine if you decided you were going to lose weight by only eating bananas for breakfast, lunch, and dinner. How long would you last on that diet before you got sick of bananas?

If you despise writing, starting a blog is probably a bad idea. If you are painfully shy on video or hate the sound of your recorded voice, online video or podcasting will be hard to sustain.

How do you know what you might be good at and enjoy doing?

In Chapter 10, we talked about how to pick platforms for social media efforts. That decision needs to go hand in hand with determining what type of content you might want to produce... or whether you might want to consider *curating* content instead.

11.5 Why Curation Might Be Better Than Creation

On YouTube alone, more than 300 hours of content are uploaded every 60 minutes. Rather than creating more content to add to the noise, sometimes the best way to stand out is to find the best *existing* content and share it with your audience.

> Content curation is the act of gathering and sharing the best information on any topic.

One way to tell if you might have an opportunity to curate information is by looking at the volume of content available about your industry. If you are a financial advisor, for example, the Internet is filled with advice of questionable value. What would you tell your clients to pay attention to and what should they ignore?

In a situation like this, the greatest value you could provide might come from helping current and prospective customers filter out the inaccurate or outdated content and pay attention only to what matters.

11.6	**The Non-Obvious Content Marketing Library**

The irony of writing this chapter is that I have far more content about content marketing than almost any other topic. It is far too much to squeeze into a book like this.

For that reason, I worked to build a robust online resources section with much more detail on specific tactics mentioned in this chapter. In the tutorial, you will find advice on everything from creating a content calendar to a 90-day plan for starting a blog.

VISIT ONLINE RESOURCES FOR:
A collection of tutorials on writing a blog and more.

**CHAPTER SUMMARY
KEY TAKEAWAYS:**

- Create content to answer the most common questions your audience asks.

- Don't treat every social media platform equally— figure out where you will focus.

- Use content curation to avoid adding to the noise online and gathering the best content instead.

Chapter 12

How to Work with Influencers

In 1905, a controversial scientific theory that should have been widely ignored was published in a small German publication called *Annalen der Physik*. The only reason it attracted any attention at all was thanks to the support of Max Planck.

As one of the most renowned scientists of his time, Planck decided to introduce the theory and its unorthodox author to the closed and highly critical world of established science. That was the way the world would first discover an unknown patent clerk named Albert Einstein and his special theory of relativity.

Planck's door-opening endorsement earned Einstein immediate credibility and gave his ideas the platform they needed to change the world.

Einstein never would have become *Einstein* without Planck's support.

Planck was an influencer, and his service as a mentor and champion made a huge difference in Einstein's life. What if you could find influencers like that and enlist their help to promote your business to the world?

That is the topic we will explore in this chapter.

12.1	**Who Is an Influencer?**

When you hear the word *influencer*, you may think of an entertainment celebrity or a social media star or a well-known industry analyst. These people certainly qualify, but influencers can come in many other varieties as well.

> In the right situation, anyone can be an influencer.

In the context of marketing, an influencer is someone who has the ability to persuade or affect the beliefs or purchasing decisions of your target audience.

Broadly defined, influencers fit into four categories:

1. **Industry influencers:** These are experts such as analysts, authors, academics, and anyone else who shares expertise publicly with others in your industry.

2. **Cultural influencers:** This group might range from actors and musicians to YouTube or social media stars who have built large, loyal followings.

3. **Media influencers:** These types work in media and include bloggers, podcast hosts, and journalists.

4. **Employee + partner influencers:** This group includes people who work for you and partners who work with you. They are often close to your business and offer an insider's point of view.

Which category of influencer should you focus on first? The answer lies with your customers. Who influences their purchasing decisions?

VISIT ONLINE RESOURCES FOR:
Advice on working with influencers for marketing.

The following story is an example of how you can find and engage an influencer effectively.

CASE STUDY: ENGAGING SNEAKERHEADS

Soon after turning 13, my son declared himself a "sneakerhead." The term is used to describe collectors who make a hobby (and sometimes a profession) out of collecting high-end sneakers made by brands like Adidas, Nike, New Balance, and Reebok.

There was a new sneaker shop opening relatively close to our house, and part of their grand opening involved an appearance by a YouTube personality, who was giving away a pair of his shoes.

The Saturday morning of the event, I was nominated to drive my son and his friends to attend, and when we arrived, there were already fans lined up around the building. The grand opening was hours away—but they didn't mind. They were there because of the appeal of the YouTuber and were thrilled when they finally got to meet him.

The store's opening was a hit thanks to their smart use of an influencer to help spread the word among taste-making sneakerheads who would go and tell all their friends about the shop.

12.2 How to Ask for Help from Influencers

I often get requests to review products, endorse apps, make introductions, or help someone promote something—and many of these requests are ineffective. The ones that stand out, however, do follow a few basic principles:

TIP 1 BUILD THE RELATIONSHIP FIRST

When I wrote my first book, I knew I wanted author Guy Kawasaki to write the foreword. Unfortunately, I didn't know him. So I entered a presentation contest that he was judging just to get his attention. A few weeks later, I referenced the contest when I emailed him to ask if he might be open to looking at my book. He kindly agreed and eventually did the foreword as well. No one likes or responds to a person who immediately asks for a favor. You need to build a relationship first.

TIP 2 DO YOUR HOMEWORK

Nothing is worse than an irrelevant pitch or note that's clearly been sent out to a mass list. The best pitches I receive often reference a belief I share or something I am passionate about. Relevance matters, and the best way to be relevant is to do your homework and know what your influencer cares about.

TIP 3 USE NON-CREEPY CYBERSTALKING

Many influencers share their whereabouts and thoughts on social media. Pay attention and you might find a way to converse with them in real-time or maybe even in person (like at a public event). Just remember to respect some basic boundaries. For example, if an influencer tweets about having a nice meal at a local restaurant, it would probably cross the line to rush over there and say hello. Watch what they do, but don't let this turn you into a creepy cyberstalker.

TIP 4 ASK FOR SOMETHING SPECIFIC

If you don't specify what you want, you aren't going to get it. For example, asking for an influencer's help is less specific than asking whether you can send a sample of your great product for them to try without any expectations. The best requests are simple and clear, and they don't require a heavy investment of time.

TIP 5 CONNECT WITH THEIR GATEKEEPERS

Sometimes the path to reach an influencer is through their network. If they own a company, check LinkedIn to see who works for them. If they are popular on Twitter but only follow a handful of people, see the few they follow. These are the gatekeepers who may be willing to make an introduction for you if you can build a relationship with them first.

12.3 Why Brand Ambassadors Are Better Than Spokespeople

I once saw an ad for a fast-food chain that had a skinny supermodel eating a "mile-high bacon thickburger." This is a typical tactic of misleading marketing: hiring celebrities as spokespeople for products they never would use in real life.

There is one thing that is always better: having your best customers and most passionate employees share their love for your products and services in an authentic and believable way. When they do, these people become your *brand ambassadors.*

> Brand ambassadors are the people who love what you do and want to tell the world about it.

Around the time that I saw the supermodel ad with the burger, I also watched an ad for Lincoln cars. It featured actor Matthew McConaughey driving a Lincoln while speaking to the camera. In the ad, he says, "I've been driving a Lincoln long before anyone paid me to drive one. I just liked it."

I have the same sort of affection for a handful of companies. You probably do, too. The challenge is to find people who might feel like that about your business and be willing to share their passion with the rest of the world.

| 12.4 | **How to Find Your Influencers** |

Another thing to consider when looking for influencers who can help to promote your business is whether they will be online, offline, or perhaps both. Here are a few example situations that will help bring this idea to life:

→ If you are marketing a retail location, consider if you have any hotels nearby. If so, the people at the front desk of that hotel are influencers for your business because they can immediately send over customers.

→ If you are promoting a doctor's office that relies on re- ferrals from other doctors, you know that your immedi- ate influencers are the people who work in the referring doc's office and those referring doctors as well.

→ If your influencers are mostly online, you can easily use social media tools to see who has the most engagement on the topics you care about and learn whether they may be open to working with you.

→ If you are promoting a non-profit that raises funds for disease research, consider which celebrities might have a personal connection to your cause, and then share any content they might have already produced about it so you can get on their radar and start to build a relationship with them directly (or with their people, if they happen to be a big celebrity).

**CHAPTER SUMMARY
KEY TAKEAWAYS:**

- An influencer Is someone who has the ability to affect the purchasing decisions of your audience.

- The best influencers are not always famous, but they always have the trust of their audience.

- The ideal way to engage an influencer is to build a relationship first and ask for help later.

Chapter 13

How to Master Search Marketing

If you have ever planned a trip to Greece, Matt Barrett probably helped you figure out where to go.

For the past 22 years, Matt has been writing a comprehensive travel guide (www.greecetravel.com) for the country he loves. He has no staff, his website has more than 5,000 pages, and the design has remained mostly unchanged for two decades.

Thanks to his long tenure and volumes of frequently updated content, Matt dominates search engine traffic for tourism to Greece. His site ranks in the top ten for every relevant keyword. Whether you are thinking of honeymooning in Santorini or looking for great experiences for kids in Athens, you are likely to find the information you need on his website.

Many businesses would do almost anything to have this kind of search engine dominance. In Matt's case, it took decades and an ongoing passion for providing the best content about Greece on the Internet.

How can you achieve a great search presence without 20 years and thousands of pages of content to build from? In this chapter, we will answer this question by learning the basics of search marketing and how to make your business more visible online.

13.1 | The Elements of Search Marketing

There are two sides to search marketing: paid search and organic search.

Paid search refers to a method of selecting keywords or phrases from a platform like Google and paying advertising fees to appear in the results when someone searches for those words. Paid search is also known as **Search Engine Marketing (SEM)**.

Organic search refers to how search engines' algorithms allow people to find your site based on the relevance of your content. To affect this type of search and rank higher, you need to use **Search Engine Optimization (SEO)**.

So which one should you do? The best approach usually starts with a combination of both.

<table>
<tr><td>13.2</td><td># How to Find the Best Keywords (and Phrases)</td></tr>
</table>

13.2 How to Find the Best Keywords (and Phrases)

No matter what you do with search, everything starts with the use of the right keywords. What words or phrases are people using that relate to your business? The answer determines how you buy your advertising or optimize your website's content.

Here are a few techniques to start building your list of keywords and doing some keyword research:

1. **Focus on phrases, not keywords:** If you needed advice on what to do with kids on a lazy summer day and you simply typed "summer activity" into Google, you would most likely get a lot of irrelevant results. Instead, if you typed "best summer activity for kids in Toronto," you would likely get better and more useful results.

2. **Use professional tools:** Tools like Google's Keyword Planner help you see search trends, get keyword suggestions, and learn what phrases are most popular in terms of search volume.

3. **Track your competitors:** When you search for common keywords or phrases, do your competitors' ads appear? If so, what language and common words do they use, and are they compelling? Can you learn anything from their ads that you could repurpose?

13.3	SEO: How to Improve Your Search Ranking

Because SEO is always changing, ranking well for a keyword today is no guarantee that you will remain highly ranked tomorrow. However, you can follow some general principles for making your site as search-engine-friendly as possible.

1. **Consistently update your content:** Search engines reward sites with recent content. The more consistently you add updated content with keywords and phrases your audience cares about, the more your site will appear in search results.

2. **Get other sites to link to you:** Search engines prioritize sites that have many other sites linking to them. They assume that if other sites are linking to yours, then your content must be good.

3. **Improve the number of clicks via search results:** Google's machine-learning algorithm (known as RankBrain) looks for pages that have lots of visits. Better page titles and descriptions can help you increase the number of people who click on a search result to end up on your site.

4. **Use images and video:** With integrated search results, video and images are presented alongside text results. Optimizing images and videos for search is something many people don't do. If you can do it, you can stand out and rank higher.

VISIT ONLINE RESOURCES FOR:
Advice, tools, and resources to do search marketing.

13.4	SEM: How to Run a Paid Search Marketing Campaign

When it comes to running a paid search marketing campaign, most platforms like Google offer step-by-step instructions for creating a campaign yourself. There is no need to repeat all those details here, so let's talk about a few basics you should know before beginning your search marketing efforts.

TIP 1 KNOW YOUR MATCH TYPES

Google allows you to set your keywords by match type, which essentially means that you can pick what type of search will cause your ad to appear. Here's a handy table to illustrate the differences:

Adwords Keyword Match Types

MATCH TYPE	SPECIAL SYMBOL	EXAMPLE KEYWORD	ADS MAY SHOW ON SEARCHES THAT	EXAMPLE SEARCHES
Broad Match	None	soccer shoes	Include misspellings, synonyms, related searches, and other relevant variations	buy football cleats
Broad Match Modifier	+ keyword	+soccer +shoes	Contain the modified term (or closer variations, but not synonyms), in any order	shoes for soccer
Phrase Match	"keyword"	"soccer shoes"	Are a phrase and close variations of that phrase	buy soccer shoes
Exact Match	(keyword)	(soccer shoes)	Are an exact term and close variations of that exact term	soccer shoes

TIP 2 USE SPLIT TESTS

A split test allows you to run two different ads against the same group of keywords to see which one performs better and gets more clicks. This can help focus your efforts and put more budget into the ad that is working best.

TIP 3 TARGET THE SECOND OR THIRD SPOT

While there is often intense and expensive competition to buy the number-one search result for a popular keyword, taking the number-two or -three slot can be far cheaper. For example, a top spot might require a bid of $10 per click, but the second spot might cost only $1.51 per click because you just need to bid slightly more than the current number-two result in order to displace them and have your ad show up second instead.

TIP 4 GO BEYOND GOOGLE

Should you advertise on any site other than Google? It can be worth experimenting with other platforms such as Bing or Yahoo. As you run ads, you can test the conversion rates to measure how those placements are working and use the data to decide whether it is worth continuing.

TIP 5 ENGAGE A COPYWRITER

As with most online ads, you have a limited amount of space to make an impact. If you are a writer, great! If you're not, this is a good place to bring in some professional help to make your ads as compelling as possible.

**CHAPTER SUMMARY
KEY TAKEAWAYS:**

- Search marketing is all about keywords and key phrases. Focus on what people actually search for.

- Paid search is SEM and allows you to pay for ads to show up against select keywords or phrases.

- Organic search is impacted by SEO, a way of optimizing content to rank higher on search results.

Chapter 14

How to Use Email and Direct-Response

The most famous crystal bowl in the world takes five years to make.

Glass cutters in the apprentice program at the renowned Waterford Crystal factory in Ireland learn how to make a

This is the handmade Waterford Apprentice bowl

variety of cuts for everything from sculptures to wine glasses. At the end of their training, the final step before apprentices graduate is to make a crystal Apprentice Bowl (pictured) that incorporates every cut they have learned.

While cutting and carving that bowl doesn't take five years, acquiring the skills required to make it does. This is how mastery works: You start with basics and build your knowledge until you achieve expert status.

With marketing, sometimes it seems as if the opposite is true.

The more we hear about new social media and big data gathering that allow us to reach people with laser-like precision, the less we expect that older, more "traditional" types of marketing can work.

Who would buy something from an infomercial anymore? Or pay for a print ad in a catalog or phone book? Or send people unsolicited mail? Or blast them with email? These are all forms of direct-response marketing, and you might be surprised at just how effective they can all still be.

14.1 Why Direct Marketing Isn't Dead

One of the biggest marketing mistakes I ever made was not focusing on my email list.

For nearly a decade, my website had hundreds and sometimes thousands of visitors a day whom I never asked to join a list. By the time I finally started asking, I had missed out on collecting tens of thousands of names.

My passion for email might seem odd to you. Hasn't the rise of unwanted spam and the ease of unsubscribing meant that email has become irrelevant? No, it hasn't.

Unlike an audience on Facebook or subscribers on YouTube, an email list is an asset that you own entirely. Using such a list to communicate directly with your audience is an example of direct marketing.

You may be skeptical that direct marketing can still be worth the time and effort, but it works because of how people consume media today.

> As people get better at avoiding irrelevant messages, they also get better at discovering relevant ones.

Any Internet user today can use technology to avoid irrelevant marketing. This level of control also means that they may be more likely to pay attention to messages from a relevant source they trust.

When I get an email about a new coffee flavor from Nespresso or the latest line of luggage from Briggs & Riley, I am much more likely to click and place an order because they are brands that I like.

Political campaigns raise the lion's share of their donations directly from email. Non-profits often see similar results. Email is also the king when it comes to redemptions on sales offers from ecommerce brands.

When consumers are savvier, direct-response marketing with specific messages and offers can be more effective because the ones who choose to pay attention are the ones most likely to take advantage of the offer as well.

CASE STUDY: WARBY PARKER

Warby Parker was founded in 2010 to offer designer glasses at a price far below what most leading manufacturers were charging. Because the company sells glasses online, it needs to ask all its customers for a doctor's prescription before it can make a sale. Having that prescription means that Warby Parker not only knows what power lenses a customer needs but also when that prescription will expire.

So just before the expiration date, customers get a reminder email saying that their prescription is going to expire soon, and they might want to consider getting some new glasses along with the new prescription they need.

This is a perfect example of how to do effective email marketing: a relevant message is delivered at the right moment to an audience of consumers who are highly likely to act on it.

14.2 Five Keys to Creating Effective Email Marketing

Email marketing is a continual process of testing and optimizing. As long as you use a professional email platform, you can access data on who opens your emails and what they click on.

To improve your email marketing, here are some basic tips.

TIP 1 OBSESS OVER SUBJECT LINES

No one will open your email if the subject line isn't compelling. Test subject lines and track open rates to see what types of subjects work better.

TIP 2 DESIGN FOR MOBILE DEVICES

Many people read their email from a mobile device, so make sure that your emails are easy to read when you open them on a smaller screen.

TIP 3 MAKE CONTENT SKIMMABLE

People generally don't read email with the same level of attention as they do with other content. Counter this by making your email skimmable with short paragraphs and relevant visuals.

TIP 4 OPTIMIZE IMAGES

Large images make emails load slowly and increase the likelihood that someone will abandon your email before reading it. Make sure that your images are small enough to keep your emails loading quickly.

TIP 5 USE LANDING PAGES TO CONVERT

A landing page is a dedicated page that usually features a single offer or message. Landing pages are separate from your website and can help increase conversion because they focus a user's attention by having a single action they can take.

14.3 How to Grow Your Email List

Whether you already have a short email list or are starting a new one, there are lots of ways you can keep it growing. Here are a few of my favorite tips for building email lists.

TIP 1 USE A SIGN-UP SHEET

Whether in a store or at an event, sign people up for your list when you see them in real life.

TIP 2   OPTIMIZE YOUR WEBSITE FOR SIGN-UPS

Use your bottom footer or a bar across the top of your site to offer multiple places to sign up.

TIP 3   ADD A SIGN-UP LINK TO YOUR EMAIL SIGNATURE

Include a simple link to join your email list as part of your own email signature to remind people to join.

TIP 4   CREATE A LOYALTY OR FAN CLUB

Engage your customers in some type of loyalty program with the promise of a discount or reward as an incentive.

TIP 5   OFFER A LEAD MAGNET

This is usually a digital item that is offered free as an incentive for people to join your list. An example is an exclusive PDF download.

TIP 6   DELIVER USEFUL EXPERTISE

Share your expertise online through content (see Chapter 11 for tips on how to do this). People are much more likely to join your email list if you continually deliver value.

TIP 7   ENGAGE THEM AFTER THEY BUY

Once you have sold a product or service, use a special card in the packaging or send a useful and personalized email to thank customers for the purchase and to ask them to join your list for future content or discounts.

STORY:
THE NON-OBVIOUS INSIGHTS NEWSLETTER

One thing I regularly teach people how to do is curate ideas in order to see patterns and predict trends. The biggest challenge they often have in following that advice is figuring out what media they should be reading, listening to, or watching.

As part of the research for my book on trends, I routinely skim or read hundreds of articles online every week from many different publications. About two years ago, I started collecting the most interesting stories in any week and sharing them with a small group of clients. After several of them asked, I turned it into a weekly email to share the "most underappreciated stories of the week."

Today that email has well over 25,000 people and is growing fast. Join the list at www.rohitbhargava.com/subscribe.

VISIT ONLINE RESOURCES FOR:
Advice on platforms and techniques for email marketing.

14.4 Direct Mail, Infomercials, and Other Direct Marketing

You might wonder who actually watches ads on late-night television for making your own beef jerky at home or a set of Japanese knives that can cut through metal.

It is easy to make fun of direct-response advertising like infomercials and the people we imagine are duped by them.

Yet when we see a one-minute video as part of a Kickstarter campaign for a magical seat cushion that vibrates every time your posture needs correction, we don't consider it as an infomercial. They are more similar than we realize. Both use compelling videos with a clear call to action in an effort to get you to buy.

There is considerable science behind direct marketing because it is and always has been highly trackable. You can tell exactly who redeems an offer and what influenced them to do it.

> Direct-response marketing makes a clear offer to get consumers to immediately take a specific action.

To see how you could use direct marketing as a part of your overall marketing strategy, here is a breakdown of a few methods you might choose, along with some advice for when each might work best.

EMAIL MARKETING

Examples: Promotional emails, newsletters, announcements

Why it works: It is easy to act on and works best when sent to a pre-qualified audience that is interested in receiving promotional offers or regular insights from you.

DIRECT-RESPONSE VIDEO

Examples: Infomercials, online pitch videos, trailers with an offer or call to action

Why it works: Compelling video often shows a product in action along with the real benefits the product offers. This is paired with some type of offer or incentive, such as "buy one, get one free" or "free shipping." It works because it makes the product benefits clear and makes an offer that seems urgent to act on.

DIRECT MAIL

Examples: Postcards, letters, or other mailers physically sent

Why it works: This tactic is typically used for offers targeted to a particular region or for existing customers as an invitation to come back. Direct mail works because it offers a physical and tangible reminder.

POSTERS & OUT-OF-HOME

Examples: Posters, flyers, billboards, or other public messages with a clear call to action

Why it works: This can range from a toll-free number on a billboard to a flier with tear-off tabs. It can be effective because it has high frequency (with people passing it again and again), and it often reaches people in an idle moment such as commuting.

**CHAPTER SUMMARY
KEY TAKEAWAYS:**

- A good email list is an asset. Grow it using online and offline methods to collect names.

- Direct marketing works because it seeks a direct and measurable response from a customer.

- The subject line is the most important part of any email marketing campaign.

Chapter 15

How to Buy and Use Advertising

"Do we really need to spend money on advertising?"

This is the question I probably hear most often when talking with small business owners about their marketing strategies. If you can deliver results through word-of-mouth and content marketing, then why pay to advertise?

Advertising isn't a replacement for those things. It works best when used to add scale and momentum to what you're already doing. If you're successful, you should use advertising to grow that success to reach more of the right people. If you have people's attention, you should use advertising to amplify that attention.

> Marketing can light a spark, and advertising can provide the fuel to turn that spark into a fire.

To better understand how advertising fits into the overall mix of marketing activities, it will help to understand the four types of media that you can employ to engage people.

15.1	Understanding the Four Types of Media

The most common model for describing types of media is known as **Paid-Owned-Earned** and describes media by who controls it. I usually add a fourth lesser-known category to this model, which I call **Rented**, to refer to social media pages that you might use but don't really own.

Here is a chart with definitions for each of the four types:

THE FOUR TYPES OF MEDIA	
Paid	Any form of media that you pay for, including all forms of advertising, sponsorship, and product placement.
Owned	Any media property, such as a website or printed newsletter, that your business owns and controls.
Earned	Media in which your business is mentioned or featured without any payment involved, such as a mention in an article or local news.
Rented	Media from your pages or profiles on social media platforms, such as Facebook or Twitter, that you use but do not own.

15.2 How to Select the Right Media Channels

Media planning is the process of identifying and selecting the media channels on which to advertise. It includes deciding how much you will spend on each channel and what types of advertising placements will be used.

Here's a list of different media channels you might consider using.

MEDIA CHANNEL	EXAMPLES	WHAT YOU SHOULD KNOW
Television/Online Video	Local TV, national TV, YouTube	Visible and visual, but often filtered by consumers and hard to track specific results.
Radio/Podcasts	Local radio, satellite radio, podcasts	Can reach consumers within a few hours of shopping time (on the way to the store).
Print	Magazines, catalogs, directories, programs	Easy to buy and replicate, but generally requires more frequency before it will be efficient.
Out-of-Home	Billboards, public transit, posters	Localized and potentially disruptive. Needs good creative placement, otherwise will be ignored.
Social Media	Banners or text-based ad units	Targeted, data-centric, and economical, but requires personalization and ongoing management.
Web/Search	Banner ads or text-based ads	Targeted and highly trackable but requires constant optimization and can get expensive quickly.

Event	Conferences, seminars, trade shows	Engages people in real life, but requires strong creative and in-person resourcing/attendance.
Direct Response	Infomercials, email, direct mail	Trackable and results oriented, but can turn consumers off when done too aggressively.

This wide range of options can make media planning seem overwhelming. The best way to narrow your list and decide where to advertise is to think about your audience's media consumption habits. The best media channels are the ones where your audience spends the most time.

CASE STUDY: VAIL RESORTS

Vail Ski Resorts are among the busiest in the United States. For years, they relied heavily on magazine advertising to reach travelers who carefully planned their holidays in advance.

In recent years, the resorts realized more people were booking last minute—because of the ease of booking, unpredictability of snow conditions, and now the pandemic.

This shift in consumer behavior was unlikely to be a one-time occurrence, so the team at Vail Resorts began rethinking their media planning strategy focus on real-time, last-minute deals.

The shift paid off, as their marketing spend became much more predictable and generated big results.

15.3 How to Buy (and Negotiate) Advertising

Most advertising today is sold via an outdated set of demographics-based parameters and requires that you understand acronyms like GRPs or CPMs. The first thing you should know about buying advertising is that the basic rules of pricing are similar to street markets.

> Some prices are fixed, and others are negotiable.

The fixed-price units are generally the types of advertising that you can purchase through self-service platforms like Google AdWords or Facebook. Event sponsorships or print advertising are usually negotiable because you buy them from a sales professional. The bargaining is based on how much inventory they have left and how much time they have to sell it.

To see how media negotiation works, read the following Case Study for an example.

CASE STUDY: THE $50,000 PRINT AD

Magazines and newspapers sell advertising using rate cards. Last year, I was negotiating with a large national magazine to place a full-page ad, which was listed at $50,000 on their rate card.

I didn't have that kind of budget.

Instead, I suggested that we treat the ad as a pilot, and if it worked, I would come back and spend more (which was true). The ad rep immediately suggested she could drop the price to the preferred rate for frequent advertisers: $30,000. It was still above my budget.

I shared that I might be able to get to $15,000 if they could make a one-time exception. The day before the deadline, I heard back from the ad rep. Was I still interested? At that point, I knew they had availability.

So I waited until 3 p.m. on the day of the deadline. Then I sent her one final offer: an immediate certified bank wire for $12,000, delivered before the 5 p.m. deadline, along with a promise of confidentiality.

We closed the deal.

CHAPTER SUMMARY
KEY TAKEAWAYS:

- Media planning is the process of selecting media channels, placements, and budgets.

- When placing ads, make sure you know which prices are fixed and which are negotiable.

- Media can be divided into the following categories: paid, owned, earned, and rented.

Chapter 16

How to Generate Publicity That Matters

When marketing consultant Ryan Holiday created a promotional plan for a film about drinking and sexual conquests titled *I Hope They Serve Beer in Hell*, his strategy hinged on classic reverse psychology: Get young men to see the film by telling them not to.

Holiday sent fake tips to gullible media properties like Gawker and made intentionally offensive ads to anger (mostly) female reporters and bloggers.

Holiday later recalled:

> *"My favorite was the campaign in Chicago...after placing a series of offensive ads on buses and the metro, from my office I alternated between calling in angry complaints to the Chicago CTA and sending angry emails to city officials with reporters cc'd, until 'under pressure,' they announced that*

> *they would be banning our advertisements and*
> *returning our money. Then we put out a press*
> *release denouncing this cowardly decision. I've*
> *never seen so much publicity. It was madness."[7]*

The movie's opening was much larger than expected. Holiday would go on to write a best-selling book called *Trust Me, I'm Lying*, to offer a transparent exposé of how the media works and what it takes to manipulate their attention.

The underlying message of Holiday's book is that there is a formula for how media operates today, and learning how it works can help you generate attention for whatever you are selling.

16.1　The Two Sides of Publicity

Public relations (often shortened to PR) describes the practice of shaping the perception of a company or individual in the eyes of both the media and the public.

This chapter will cover two forms of publicity that you can generate with PR:

1. **Earned media:** Attention and coverage from the mainstream media, typically in the form of articles, stories, mentions, or features.

2. **User-generated content (UGC):** Coverage from individuals online, including everything from blog posts and videos to online reviews.

To start, earned media can provide a good launching pad for your business because it helps you scale attention without having to spend on advertising. To do it well, a good place to start is by looking at the work of the "Godfather of persuasion," Dr. Robert Cialdini.

16.2   The Six Principles of Persuasion

Cialdini's book, *Influence: The Psychology of Persuasion,* was first published in 1984 and is widely considered among the best business books ever written. In it, he introduces six essential principles of persuasion: reciprocity, scarcity, authority, consistency, liking, and consensus.

THE SIX PRINCIPLES OF PERSUASION	
Reciprocity	People feel obliged to give back to others in the form of a behavior, gift, or service that they have received first.
Scarcity	People want more of those things they can have less of.
Authority	People follow the lead of credible, knowledgeable experts.
Consistency	People like to be consistent with the things they have previously said or done.
Liking	People prefer to say yes to those that they like.
Consensus	Especially when they are uncertain, people will look to the actions and behaviors of others to determine how they too should act.

Once you read these principles, you may start to spot them in action all around you:

→ Restaurants use *authority* by featuring framed reviews from newspapers on their walls to reinforce that the food must be good because a noted critic enjoyed dining there.

→ Retail stores offer free samples to exercise the principle of *reciprocity*. Receiving a free sample makes us more likely to buy that product.

→ Any time you see a message in an online store saying there are "Only 3 left in stock!"—it's an example of the principle of *scarcity* at work.

→ The principle of *consensus* means that you are likely to expect a positive experience from a business if you see positive online reviews about it.

→ My business card includes the tagline "nice guy." This was inspired by the principle of *liking* and helps me offer a reminder to anyone I meet that I'm easy to collaborate with.

→ When a telemarketer asks you if you care about a certain issue, they are usually trying to employ the principle of *consistency*. If you say yes, they know you're far more likely to agree to make a donation so you'll remain consistent with your stated beliefs.

16.3 How to Generate Earned Media

The principles of persuasion are the perfect starting point for you to generate publicity because they offer a good framework for engaging reporters and the media. Let's see how this can work.

TIP 1 OFFER EXPERIENCES OF VALUE

I have been to dozens of media events, and they usually offer attendees media kits and gift bags with product samples and other items. These sometimes include a collection of images on a USB stick or a book to review, or products to try. These gifts increase the likelihood that media may offer a mention fueled by the principle of *reciprocity*.

TIP 2   MAKE IT AN EXCLUSIVE

PR pros frequently employ a technique in which they offer media an exclusive story, meaning no other news outlet can cover it, in exchange for the promise that the story will be featured prominently. This application of the principle of *scarcity* can maximize your chances of generating earned media attention, too, as long as the "exclusive" you are offering is interesting and newsworthy.

VISIT ONLINE RESOURCES FOR:
A glossary of media terms and advice on buying advertising.

TIP 3   BE AN EXPERT

Whether you know the difference between Brazilian and Italian granite or how to make a perfect espresso, your expertise can be the biggest selling point you have. Content marketing and direct outreach to media can help you get on their radar and offer yourself as an expert source.

TIP 4   KNOW THE PERSON

Don't blast out a one-size-fits-all press release. Do some research. Learn what a reporter or influencer cares about and the "beat" (topic) that they cover. Then tailor your pitch to make them care.

CASE STUDY:
HOW TO EXECUTE A PR CAMPAIGN

Imagine you are putting together a product marketing program for a new pillow. How would you get attention from the media and the public? Here are some examples of PR tactics:

→ Announce "National Pillow Day," where people are encouraged to rage online about how much they hate their current pillows. If they tag a photo online with your campaign hashtag #hatemypillow, they can earn a discount on a new pillow.

→ Invite journalists and bloggers to an exclusive "Pillow Breakfast," where they have breakfast in bed catered by a well-known chef while trying out your pillows.

→ Launch a "trade in your pillow" offer for Valentine's Day.

→ Go to a large trade show and try to introduce your pillow as a contender for the "most innovative product" winner in a relevant category.

→ Find a dating coach/expert and hire him or her to host a "Pillow Talk Podcast," where you share advice on how to meet that special someone.

→ Partner with a small group of universities to create a "Student Sleep Survey," where you measure how sleep affects school performance.

TIP 5   TRACK EDITORIAL CALENDARS

Larger publications are put together weeks or months in advance. Most of them will publish an editorial calendar that lists what they will be writing about in upcoming issues. Think of it as a sneak peek into what stories will get published and an invaluable source in shaping your pitch for those stories because you know the themes and topics reporters will be most interested in.

VISIT ONLINE RESOURCES FOR:
Advice on PR and generating publicity.

TIP 6   BUILD PERSONAL CONNECTIONS

The cliché of "it's not who you know, it's who knows you" still applies in the world of media. The more personal connections you establish with journalists, the more likely you are to be featured in a story. To plant the seed, reach out on social media like LinkedIn and Twitter and offer them your expertise. Or find out where they will be speaking at or attending an event so you can try to meet them in person.

CASE STUDY: THE AUSTRALIAN CROCODILE ATTACK

"Newsjacking" is a term that author David Meerman Scott first used to describe "the art and science of injecting your ideas into a breaking news story and generating tons of media coverage and social media engagement."

One example he regularly shares is a small Australian insurance company that took advantage of then president Obama's visit to the country. They shared a blog post offering the president and his wife free insurance in the unlikely event of a crocodile attack. Nearly 5,000 news media articles about Obama's visit that week included mention of this clever stunt, generating a ton of publicity for the insurance company.

16.4	How to Encourage Positive User-Generated Content

Let's look at how to inspire customers to create positive user-generated content.

TIP 1   LET PEOPLE KNOW IT MATTERS

I remember getting into an Uber ride where the driver had a sign detailing why five-star reviews mattered and why a four-star rating was worse than no review at all because of how it affected his overall score. Most of the time customers don't realize the impact (positive or negative) that a review can make, so educating them can make a big difference. He got five stars from me.

TIP 2   GET A VERBAL COMMITMENT

When people make a promise to do something, they are much more likely to follow through (thanks to the principle of consistency). For this reason, telemarketers try to get you to commit to donating money or buying a product on the phone. The same principle can work for user-generated content.

TIP 3   INVITE PEOPLE TO SHARE AN EXPERIENCE

While some people may be reluctant to share a written review, they may be happy to share their experience through photos and videos posted on social media, so ask for that instead.

TIP 4   CREATE CAPTURE MOMENTS

Driving along the highway, people stop at scenic overlooks and take photos as a reminder to enjoy the experience. If you can help your customers find their own special moments when using your products or services, you greatly increase the chances they will take that content and share it.

TIP 5   ASK NICELY!

When someone has a truly amazing experience and has a personal connection to you, sometimes all it takes to get the person to create content about it is remembering to ask.

**CHAPTER SUMMARY
KEY TAKEAWAYS:**

- There are two types of publicity—earned media and user-generated content (UGC).

- Positive earned media or UGC can help underscore why customers should trust you.

- There are six principles of persuasion: reciprocity, scarcity, authority, consistency, liking, and consensus.

Chapter 17

How to Do Event and Trade Show Marketing

Every year I speak at and attend about 40 conferences and trade shows (and over the past year, this number has ballooned to more than a hundred when you consider all the virtual events!), which means I probably have interacted with thousands of vendors in exhibit hall booths, real and virtual, over the past few years.

I believe 80 percent of them are wasting their money, and that estimate is probably low.

The sad fact is that many companies are buying a ten-by-ten-foot space, having a few branded pens printed with their logo, and hoping to meet buyers or others who will have an impact on their business.

The good thing about events is that you have the right people in the right place at a time when they are ready to buy. The bad news is that there is lots of competition for their attention.

How can you stand out at a trade show, and how do you decide whether to go at all?

In this chapter, you will learn about marketing at an event (real-life or virtual!) and what it really takes to create an engaging booth experience and even get on stage as a speaker.

17.1 How to Stand Out at Any Trade Show

At the largest trade show in the world, it is hard to stand out. When I join more than 50,000 participants every January in Las Vegas at the Consumer Electronics Show (CES), I always seek out marketing ideas that work. Here are a few of my favorites.

TIP 1 FIND PARTNERS WITH DEEPER POCKETS

One year at CES, I met a start-up that created interactive display walls. That year, American Airlines was using the start-up's platform to power a part of its huge booth in the middle of the convention center. The visibility of that placement and the big brand showcase for the technology helped the start-up attract a lot of attention.

TIP 2   FIND AN UNEXPECTED MOMENT

At many large events, there are big parties with long lines to get in. One year, a business that made screen protectors for cell phones sent a street team out to approach people in line for a party and ask them to try the new product and post about it on social media. The team had the perfect captive audience, and people loved the idea of getting extra screen protection before heading out for a night of partying. The promotion was a big hit.

TIP 3   BE WHERE YOUR COMPETITORS AREN'T

At a typical trade show, dozens of booths are lined up side by side, which makes it harder to stand out. I once had an engaging conversation with a vendor who was standing in the main hallway of the exhibit hall, meeting people and showcasing his product. It worked because he broke out of the confines of his booth and literally stood out.

TIP 4   GO BEYOND BOOTH BABES

One tired tactic from the past is to hire young, attractive women to work at your booth. These so-called "booth babes" are meant to draw a mainly male audience. At CES, this tactic did attract attention momentarily, but I witnessed most people moving along quickly and giving little notice to the company behind the booth. More significantly, the company probably alienated female prospective buyers and customers.

TIP 5   REACH OUT TO INFLUENCERS

It can pay off to identify the influencers you want to meet who will be attending or speaking at an event. Once you know when and where they will appear, you can plan to attend, introduce yourself afterward, and make a personal connection.

TIP 6   SPEND ON THE GIVEAWAYS, NOT THE BOOTH

Nothing spreads faster at a trade show than word of mouth about a great giveaway. When tech device company Jawbone first came to CES, they had a tiny booth. Instead of investing in a costly booth design, they offered an innovative trade-in to exchange your old Bluetooth headset for a new Jawbone, valued at $119 retail. The offer created huge buzz and led to long lines of people excited to upgrade their headsets.

Here are a few of the popular giveaways we have used in the past.

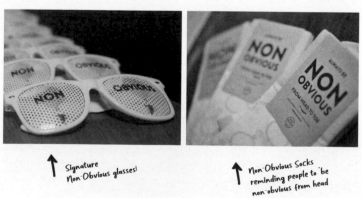

↑ Signature
Non-Obvious glasses!

↑ Non-Obvious Socks
reminding people to be
non-obvious from head
to toe!

STORY: THE NON-OBVIOUS BOOTH EXPERIENCE

A few months before the pandemic, my team and I decided to exhibit at the SHRM trade show, an event for human resources professionals.

In addition to giving away signed books, we had two other giveaways.

One was bright yellow tweezers with the tagline "Non-Obvious Innovation Raises Eyebrows!" We knew that one would be a big hit with the audience, which skewed about 70 percent female.

The other was a collection of candy from all the countries our team had done consulting in, which we called the "Non-Obvious Candy Collection."

The candy and tweezers drove lots of word of mouth. By the end of the event, we connected with more than a thousand HR managers—over twice what we had hoped for.

17.2   How to Speak at an Event

Are you willing to go on stage in front of a group of people and talk about your business and your expertise?

Speaking on stage sounds scary, but if you can conquer your nerves, it can be a fantastic way to promote your business by helping you quickly gain the respect of other attendees (not to mention earning you a free pass to the event).

The easiest way to start speaking on stage is to join a panel. Here's how to do it:

1. Find an event where you would like to speak.

2. Review the list of panels available and identify which ones have a topic you could contribute to.

3. Check the maximum number of people listed on any panel at the event. (It is usually five.)

4. See how many speakers are listed. If it is less than five, that panel may have space for one more.

5. Find the name of the moderator (usually listed) and contact that person directly. Suggest yourself as a panelist and summarize the unique perspective you would bring.

6. After you secure a panelist slot, check if the event can cover your travel or other expenses. It never hurts to ask!

| 17.3 | **How to Be Great at Networking (Even If You Hate It)*** |

Many people dread networking events. The idea of having to make small talk and hand out business cards to sell yourself to strangers is hard. Yet you know your network matters, so going to these events seems like a necessary evil. How can you navigate the awkwardness of networking and come out ahead?

TIP 1   GET IN LINE

Walking up to random people to start conversations is hard for anyone. Standing in line and striking up a conversation with the people next to you is easier because you all have a reason for being there. The longer the line, the deeper the conversation you can have. And if it's not going well, you can excuse yourself to head to the bathroom!

*Note—This section was originally written before the pandemic. See the next section for advice on creating and succeeding in virtual events.

TIP 2 BRING AN OUTGOING FRIEND

Bringing an outgoing friend to an event can be a great way to meet people because your friend does most of the work. If you happen to be that outgoing friend, be generous with your time and help your quieter counterparts out!

TIP 3 ASK INTRIGUING QUESTIONS

Asking people where they are from or what their job is guarantees an ordinary conversation. Instead, try to ask more intriguing questions. For example, ask what their passion is or how they decided to do what they do. Better questions = better conversations.

TIP 4 ALWAYS EAT LEFT-HANDED

This was the title of one of my previous books, and it refers to one of my favorite tactics to make networking better. Eating with my left hand made me feel more approachable because my right hand was always free to shake someone else's.

TIP 5 INTERRUPT MORE OFTEN

We all have heard the advice that we need to listen more, but often we misinterpret it to mean that we should just shut up and nod during a conversation. Great conversationalists and great interviewers practice strategic interruptions. They listen actively to conversations and often interject follow-up questions to drive the conversation forward.

TIP 6   PROACTIVELY OFFER YOUR HELP

One of the most memorable things anyone can do at a networking event is to offer to help. This most often comes with the phrase "I should introduce you to…" The people who do this are connectors, and you can be one as well.

TIP 7   FOLLOW THROUGH

Following from the previous point, during a networking event we often mention something that we will share or do, but then we forget about it. The best networkers are the ones who remember what they promise and follow through. Just doing that consistently will make you stand out because so many people don't.

17.4   How to Produce Your Own Virtual Event

With so much of our lives online, the virtual or hybrid experience you're producing must deliver true value to compete with all the other available choices. Here are some tips on how to do it.

TIP 1 PRELOAD THE FUN

When promoting a virtual event, seed messaging with a few practical insights and content-driven teasers. These can build buy-in and foster a feeling of exclusivity. That way, registrants don't just learn when your event's happening; they have even more reasons to attend.

TIP 2 PLAN CONTENT BEFORE PLATFORM

First, choose the content you want to communicate, and then choose your platform of content delivery technology.

TIP 3 START WITH THE BEST FIRST

On the day of your event, optimize attention by beginning with your very best, most enticing, carefully scripted content. Dive right into your most compelling ideas. These are never sponsor-related remarks or profuse thank-yous. If you're recording the programming, superb content ensures the footage can be used in promotional teasers for the next event. (See what you missed?!)

TIP 4 TRANSFORM PASSIVITY INTO ACTIVITY

If you're not planning to add interactivity, you should reconsider migrating online. Your "experience" may be better and more simply communicated via email. Build engagement beyond a simple chatbox by ensuring that content includes varied interactivity. Try quizzes and contests before, during, and after.

Use audience polling and integrate Q&A time and whiteboarding. Choose a platform in which your presenter can highlight and draw in real-time. Play music and video. Close with a pithy, practical summary and a strategic call to action to end on a high note.

TIP 5 REMEMBER: LESS IS MORE

Your virtual guests will remember more when you remember to keep the agenda streamlined. The best online meetings or meeting segments are short: 30 minutes or less. Focus on just two or three important messages and takeaways, and design every agenda element around those outcomes.

TIP 6 BOOST THE AFTERGLOW

After virtual or hybrid events, hold smaller online meetups so attendees can continue connecting, learning, networking, and boosting accountability. This also can enhance in-person event attendance over time as relationships crystallize.

TIP 7 DELIVER DATA-DRIVEN RESULTS

An inherent benefit of virtual events is easy tracking of virtual attendance, participant retention rates, and your most click-worthy content. Take advantage of this built-in ROI richness so you can prove value to your stakeholders and make measurable improvements over time.

TIP 8 CREATE MORE KA-CHING

Record your meatiest virtual meetings so you can reuse the footage for new hire training, social media posts, sponsor acquisition, video blogs, and **sizzle reels** that sell future events.

**CHAPTER SUMMARY
KEY TAKEAWAYS:**

- Speaking on panels is a low-pressure, high-impact way to bring visibility to your business.

- Proactively offering to help others and asking better questions will help you network.

- Trade shows can be effective, but you need a strong, creative idea to stand out.

Chapter 18

How to Measure What Matters

Avinash Kaushik, an analytics expert who works at Google, has a fun way of describing the metric called "hits," which many people still use to track the number of visits to their website. He has turned it into the acronym HITS, which he says stands for "How Idiots Track Success."

His joke is based on the fact that measuring hits only tells you how many files are downloaded from your site. An average web page has about 15 files—but most are individual images. So using hits as an indicator of website traffic is a bit like a liquor store counting every six-pack of beer sold as if it were six separate sales.

Kaushik's point is also a perfect analogy to expose a fundamental problem when it comes to tracking your marketing: it is hard to understand what the data is actually telling you.

Television advertising is priced based on the number of viewers a program attracts, even though many of those viewers don't pay attention to the ads. Print advertising in magazines is sold based on circulation, even though the number of copies that are "circulated" doesn't accurately portray the number of people who see the magazine ads.

> The fact is, a lot of marketing metrics are bullshit.

If so many metrics in marketing are useless, why do people use them? The short answer is that they are often created solely to give us the false assurance that what we are doing is working.

18.1 Are You Using Feel-Good Metrics?

A few years ago, comedian and television host Stephen Colbert was interviewing Microsoft founder Bill Gates about how heavily the Gates Foundation relies on data and analysis to allocate its spending.

In his trademark deadpan style, Colbert shared his skepticism:

> *Here's the problem I have with that. If you*
> *track the data, you see where you're doing*
> *well, you see where you don't do well, you know*
> *if you're getting better or worse. Whereas if I*
> *keep no record of what I do, I can always assume*
> *I've succeeded.*

—Stephen Colbert

A feel-good metric might seem slightly better than no metrics at all, but the problem is that focusing on the *wrong* metrics can give you a flawed perception of what actually matters. How can you train yourself to use better and more valuable measures?

Instead, thinking in terms of "hero metrics" can help.

18.2 Using Hero Metrics to See What's Working

A couple of years ago when I was doing some work for an ecommerce company, we had to develop a metrics program to help us understand what was happening on the company's site so we could figure out where to focus our marketing. Unfortunately, we had too much data.

Often the biggest challenge with marketing metrics is knowing what to ignore.

To help understand what was happening on the site and where to focus, we developed a measurement program that concentrated on only a few metrics that proved so useful, we started calling them **hero metrics**. Here are a few examples:

1. **Top referrers:** Which websites were driving the most traffic to our site?

2. **Newsletter sign-ups:** How many people signed up to get our promotional newsletter and where did they come from?

3. **Top repeat purchase:** Which products had the highest frequency of repeat purchasing?

4. **Abandonment rate:** How often were people putting an item into their online shopping cart but abandoning our site without buying?

Once we focused on these numbers, we got an idea of which products we might want to feature in online ads and which sites we might want to consider as partners. This idea of using hero metrics isn't just for online tactics either. Let's review an example from real life.

STORY: THE HELPFUL HONDA PROGRAM

One of my favorite examples of how to measure success is the Helpful Honda Dealers program, a collaboration of nearly 50 Honda dealerships based in Southern California.

The program involved sending Honda employees dressed in light-blue polo shirts out to serve in the community. They did everything from washing customers' cars to paying for parking all day in Old Town Pasadena.

The entire effort was designed to increase the likelihood that a consumer might visit a Honda dealership and consider taking a test drive. Once a customer takes a test drive (the dealerships' hero metric), the numbers show that the likelihood of that customer purchasing a car increases dramatically.

This story highlights a powerful truth behind the relationship between marketing and sales, as well as how they should ideally work together.

> The role of marketing isn't to sell a car. It is to increase visits to the dealership so salespeople can sell the car.

18.3   Five Types of Marketing Data

There are many types of metrics that you can look at in order to find your own hero metrics. In the chart below, you will see a list of various types of marketing data, including where they come from and some examples.

TYPE OF MARKETING DATA	WHERE YOU GET IT	EXAMPLES OF METRICS
Website Metrics	Data from analytics software like Google Analytics about website usage	Number of pages visited, entry and exit pages, bounce rate, top pages, conversion rate, referral sites
Sales Metrics	Data from sales registers, inventory management systems, or invoicing systems about what has sold and for how much	Sales revenue, products sold, inventory sold and remaining, repeat purchases
Advertising Metrics	Data provided by advertising partners to illustrate the effectiveness of ads that you have placed	Impressions, clicks, conversions, views, leads, subscribes, follows
Customer and Survey Metrics	Data a customer shares with you as part of a purchase, in response to a survey, or from a customer loyalty program	Name, email, interests, address, phone, gender, location, number of visits
Industry Metrics	Data from industry reports, third-party research, or outside insights	SWOT analysis against competitors, industry trends

18.4 Using the Four A's Model of Measurement

Now that we have focused on the types of data you can collect, as well as the necessity to get past "feel-good metrics," let's figure out what numbers are worth paying attention to by using what I call the four A's of measurement.

1. **Awareness:** Are the people we care about seeing our marketing, and are we making them aware of us?

2. **Advocacy:** Are our efforts engaging people to build the brand reputation we want?

3. **Action:** Is our audience taking the right actions to make a purchase or enter into our sales process?

4. **Alignment:** Are our efforts leading to a deeper loyalty or brand preference?

The downloadable template shown on the next page outlines these four metrics in greater detail and how you can measure each one.

 VISIT ONLINE RESOURCES FOR:
A downloadable template for a measurement plan that works.

THE **NON-OBVIOUS 1 PAGE** MEASUREMENT OVERVIEW

DESIRED IMPACT	WHAT CAN THIS TYPE OF METRIC TELL YOU?	SAMPLE METRICS	EXAMPLES
AWARENESS	Are the people that we care about seeing our marketing and are we positively influencing their perception of us?	• Audience Growth (Number of followers, friends or fans) • Content Frequency (Number of posts or tweets) • Content Reach (Page or profile views or estimated audience reach, online video views) • Search Visibility (impact on content ranking for keywords, search traffic) • Brand Visibility/Association (solicited or unsolicited brand visibility related to key phrases/topics)	• 28,725 followers on Twitter • 45 new employee profiles connected to corporate LinkedIn profile • 56,456 estimated social reach of FB posts • 13% rise in search visibility for top 10 keywords • Social profile appears in top 10 for xxxx keyword • 4% rise in reputation or association among consumers (survey test)
ADVOCACY	Are our efforts engaging people to build the brand reputation we want?	• Social Engagement (Number of retweets, likes, +1s, etc.) • Social Share of Voice (percentage share of voice on key topic within specific set of conversations online) • Brand Preference (positive blog/media mentions, inclusion in key industry analyst reports, etc.)	• 45 retweets of Twitter update • 13 new blog or community comments • 4 new mentions in online media or blogs • 4% rise in positive sentiment on blogs + Twitter • Mentioned in key industry analyst report
ACTION	Is our audience taking the right actions to make a purchase or enter our sales process?	• Conversions (Number of leads generated, number of forms completed, number of PDFs downloaded, job inquiries to HR, number of signups for email newsletter) • Social Sharing (Number of shares with comment, blog comments, modified tweets with comment, etc.)	• 8% reduction in support calls to call center • 489 new email newsletter subscribers • 9% increase in lead generation forms completed • 12 personalized shares of FB post
ALIGNMENT	Are our efforts leading to a deeper collaboration or brand preference?	• Recommendations (Unsolicited social reviews, analyst or media coverage, online reviews,) • Participation/Collaboration (user generated content submissions, online idea sharing, community engagement, VIP community registrations) • Retention (Participation and feedback from repeat customers, change in referrals or retention rates).	• 5 new reviews posted online • 7 user submitted innovation ideas • 87% active members in VIP community • 2% increase in monthly spend from existing customers with active social profiles

NOTE – Use this chart as a handy guide to the type of metrics you can use based on the impact that you are trying to get.

CHAPTER SUMMARY
KEY TAKEAWAYS:

- Many of the typical metrics we use are "feel-good metrics" and provide little actionable insight.

- The most useful way to use measurement is to develop selective "hero metrics" to watch.

- There are four marketing elements you can measure: awareness, advocacy, action, and alignment.

Conclusion

In the past year since the first edition of this book came out, I spoke to thousands of business professionals and students about marketing. At the end of most sessions, one question would come up more than any other: what should I start with?

Unfortunately, there isn't a single answer to that question.

Should you create a logo before building a website? Maybe, but there are plenty of successful businesses who don't. Should you spend money on a magazine ad, or focus on building an email newsletter? Either could work. Marketing often is all about tradeoffs and strategic decisions like this.

> The order in which we do things does matter. Just not in the way we often imagine.

What matters most is the strategy you pick. Remember the point I shared at the start of the book about how great restaurants don't have chicken strategies? Great businesses don't either. If there is one big lesson this book hopefully offers - it's to always start with an understanding of what makes you different and desired, and then use your marketing strategy and tactics to tell that story.

> Marketers are storytellers. And storytellers change the world.

Good luck on your own journey in using marketing to craft your story and share it with the world. I believe taking the time to do this will help you create a powerful and memorable impact on the people you most want to reach, no matter what you do.

Endnotes

1. **Banner Blindness (Pg. 1)**—I first encountered this study when writing my thesis on UI design back in 1998, and it stuck with me. You can read the full paper at http://bit.ly/nog-bannerblindness.

2. **EL Ideas Restaurant (Pg. 11)**—This story is based on a visit I made to the restaurant in June of 2018, as well as a published story about Foss on Eater.com, titled "No Chef in America Cooks Dinner Quite Like Philip Foss." Read the story at http://bit.ly/nog-foss.

3. **Blu Homes (Pg. 23)**—Blu Homes' discovery of their true target audience was shared directly by Maura McCarthy in an article written for Inc. Read her story at http://on.inc.com/2xt1PiB.

4. **Kikkoman Documentary (Pg. 65)**—Kikkoman first released this documentary back in 2012. It was directed by Academy Award—nominated filmmaker Lucy Walker, and you can watch the full 24-minute film here: https://youtu.be/zF8GfajCtgM.

5. **Purple Mattress (Pg. 74)**—The numbers and details shared about the rise of Purple Mattress were collected from several online sources. To learn more about the story of Purple's marketing, visit this link: http://bit.ly/nog-purplemattress.

6. **Zenith Media Report** (**Pg. 89**)—To read the full report referenced here, visit http://bit.ly/nog-zenithmedia.

7. **Ryan Holiday** (**Pg. 151**)—In addition to reading Holiday's excellent book, his article written for Observer.com on how his ideas have been used by those with evil intentions (and how to avoid falling for their trap) is a worthwhile read. See the full article here: http://bit.ly/nog-ryanholiday.

Index

About the Author

Rohit Bhargava is on a mission to help the world be more open-minded by teaching others how to be non-obvious thinkers. He is the founder of the Non-Obvious Company and an entertaining, original, and "non-boring" keynote speaker on innovation and trust. He previously spent 15 years in leadership roles at two renowned ad agencies: Leo Burnett and Ogilvy. Rohit is the *Wall Street Journal* best-selling author of 7 books and has been invited to deliver keynote presentations in 32 countries around the world. His insights have been used by the World Bank, NASA, Intel, Disney, Colgate Swissotel, Coca-Cola, Schwab, Under Armour, NBC Universal, American Express, and hundreds of others to win the future. Rohit is a popular Adjunct Professor of Marketing and Storytelling at Georgetown University and also writes a monthly column for *GQ* magazine in Brazil. He believes in listening before talking, is a lifelong lover of the Olympics, and lives and works with his wife and two boys just outside Washington, D.C.

Get new ideas to help you win the future!

JOIN MY FREE EMAIL NEWSLETTER:

www.rohitbhargava.com/subscribe

Every week you will get a curated email featuring the most interesting and underappreciated stories of the week—along with short insights on what they mean for you.